Lawrence Zeegen with revisions by Louise Fenton

The Fundamentals of Illustration

2nd edition

Ethical: awareness/ reflection/ ion/ debate

ava academia

Contents

Chapter 1
The illustrator as artist
14

Chapter 4
Communicating ideas
94

Chapter 5
Making it happen
124

Chapter 2
The medium is the message
28

Chapter 3
From outcomes to outlets
54

Chapter 6
Production
150

Foreword

You enter a large, dark room and feel for the light. You find a bank of switches – row upon row. You switch one at random – a light illuminates a clean sheet of white paper lying untouched on the table. You try another – a biro doodle on the back of an envelope. Next, light falls on a scientific diagram. A further switch, surprisingly, turns on a projector and an animation starts rolling. You switch on others and a children's book appears, a single tiny postage stamp, a framed drawing hanging on the wall, a row of labelled wine bottles, a poster, a map, a comic, a model stage set and a wood engraving. A computer screen lights up. An exquisite alphabet appears. A further switch reveals a group of 3D characters. The next, a drawing of a pair of shoes in a magazine.

The last switch shines a spotlight onto the switchboard. Each switch has a label: Communication. Opinion. Drawing. Narrative. Pattern. Idea. Fashion. Movement. Promotion. Media. Recompense. Style. Tax. Composition. Sequence. Abstraction. Education. Collection. Medium.

The door to this mysterious and exciting room, like the cover of this book, has the word 'Illustration' lettered on it. Underneath, in brackets, you read, 'To illuminate or cast light on a subject'. Lawrence Zeegen has succeeded in doing just this in an intelligent, elegant and original way. Using examples that will stand the test of time, he casts light on the professionalism, philosophy and practicality of this vast subject.

Professor George Hardie

How to get the most out of this book

The Fundamentals of Illustration is intended as a comprehensive guide for illustrators, designers and those who commission illustration. It is hoped that the information provided here will encourage, inspire and inform those that are new to the subject to enjoy and thrive in the exciting and creative world of illustration.

Brainstorming

Once in possession of a fully formed project brief, notes and interpretations from the briefing meeting, a sketchbook with early inspirations and thoughts, research into the subject area as well as a project file and a fully functioning creative environment to work in, it's time to start formulating some ideas!

Brainstorming can mean different things to different people. Simply expressed, it is the action of bringing together all of the research, notes, scribbles and thoughts and creating a series of bigger and more clearly defined ideas and paths to follow. Illustrators, unlike designers, will often have to brainstorm alone – illustration can be a lonely pursuit; as a solo activity there is only one person responsible for the final outcome. Of course, working with an art director or designer on a project can help, and discussing ideas should be very much part of the process, but ultimately there is only one person creating the initial ideas – you, the illustrator.

An onslaught of ideas and thoughts is the best way to describe how brainstorming should work. Get every idea and thought out and onto paper or screen. Keep your ideas flowing – good ideas, bad ideas, exciting, dull – let them all out. Just like a storm of heavy rain and gusting wind, your brain should be working overtime to produce as much as it can. Examine possibilities, explore links, twist meanings and subvert thoughts – anything goes. To make brainstorming work, you need to have the germs of ideas and lots of them.

4.8

AUTHOR TIP:
HISTORICAL RESEARCH

– Historical accuracy may not be a factor in most illustrations, but whenever a project calls for detailed visual information about a subject, it is wise to undertake some in-depth research.
– Using expert information from reliable sources will ensure that mistakes are not made.

1. Text

Text is broken down into manageable chunks, allowing the reader to dip in and out of the book wherever they please.

2. Images

Images from a variety of sources are accompanied by captions.

3. Navigation

A navigation bar allows the reader to see which section they are currently in as well as previous sections and sections to come.

4. Author tip boxes

Author tip boxes offer additional snippets of information useful to the reader.

5. Try it yourself…

Each chapter concludes with a 'Try it yourself…' activity and a series of questions in summary.

6. Practitioner interviews

Chapter 3 offers a series of interviews with practising illustrators.

7. Case studies

Each chapter includes a practitioner case study, enabling the reader to see how a practising illustrator has approached and completed a real-life illustration project.

Introduction

Illustration is a dirty word, or at least was until recently. Neither truly accepted by the art establishment, nor the design industry, illustration has battled on regardless. Derided as whimsical by artists and as arty by designers, illustration has found itself existing in a no-man's land between the two. In education the discipline has fared no better, rarely given more than just studio space, the student illustrator has learnt to bend the rules and break across borders to gain access to facilities and equipment to facilitate their work. Life as an illustrator is not for the faint-hearted and it takes massive determination to face the demands and rigours of a career choice that can feel vastly undersupported. But, against these odds, the discipline has mounted an impressive return to form – but how, and why?

According to the National Museum of Illustration in Rhode Island, USA, 'illustrators combine personal expression with pictorial representation in order to convey ideas' – a useful description certainly, but one that falls short of fully capturing the essence of what the subject is or has been about. Describing the 'golden era', when magazines such as the *Saturday Evening Post* scoured the studios for great illustrators, the design writer and art director Steven Heller stated that 'illustration was the people's art'. This sentiment was echoed by the National Museum of Illustration: 'illustration serves as a reservoir of our social and cultural history', even going on to state, 'illustration is therefore a significant and enduring art form'.

It is illustrated images that capture the imagination, that remain with the viewer and that inextricably tie moments in one's personal history with the present. From the moment that small children are introduced to illustrated books through to their admiring record and CD sleeves in their teens and early twenties, illustrations play a part in defining important moments and periods in time. On a grander scale, it is fair to say that illustration has recorded man's achievements, interpreting them in a way not possible before the birth of photography. 'Look at the paintings of Pompeii', stresses Milton Glaser – cofounder of Pushpin Studios in New York in *The Education of the Illustrator* – 'the Aboriginal wall paintings of Australia, the great frescoes of Italy, and you understand a moment of time, and the belief systems of the population'. Contemporary illustration may work in less majestic surroundings, but its roots within the magazine racks, bookshelves and record collections of our homes stand as testament to the importance we place on the art and craft of the discipline.

Finding the exact point in time that contemporary illustration was kick-started is not an easy task. The very term 'contemporary' implies modern, current, up-to-date, fashionable and present-day, so peering too far back into a dim and distant past may draw into the frame images that today's audience would struggle to recognize or remember. If a line is drawn in the sand marking the halfway point in the last century, for example, classic illustrated posters for the Second World War campaign by Tom Eckersley, or his amazing posters for Guinness, have to be ignored, having been created in the 1940s. The same treatment must then be applied to much of the work of Abram Games, although his iconic posters for the London Underground would slip into the list, having been produced in the early 1950s. Norman Rockwell's work for the *Saturday Evening Post* in the US would have to be refused entry, as would Ben Shahn's Second World War posters. Saul Steinberg's work for *New Yorker* magazine, having emigrated to New York in 1951 from Bucharest via Milan, would make the grade, as would Edward Bawden's London Underground posters and Ronald Searle's illustrations for *Punch* magazine in the UK. For many that grew up in the 1960s and 1970s, however, the first truly contemporary illustrators came from a new generation of image-makers.

The 1960s witnessed an unprecedented rise in consumerism as the post-war 'baby boomers' approached life with an optimism and enthusiasm not seen before. Teenagers came of age: youth movements sprang up and with them the need for a graphic visual language to identify with. Psychedelia, Op Art and Pop Art all put the visual arts firmly on the map. Here was the start of a fresh, forward-thinking new era and illustrated images helped in defining the look of the decade.

It was probably The Beatles that gave popular culture during the sixties some of its most memorable illustrative images; from the Klaus Voormann sleeve for *Revolver* in 1965, to the animated classic of 'Yellow Submarine' created from Heinz Edelmann's original drawings and on to the must-have book, *The Beatles Illustrated Lyrics* by Alan Aldridge published in 1969. It was, however, the use of artist and illustrator, Peter Blake, in 1967, who combined a photographic and illustrative approach for the creation of the sleeve for *Sgt. Pepper's Lonely Heart Club Band* that ensured the Beatles' status as forward-thinking creative directors as well as musicians.

Iconic illustrated images that mark the 1960s out as being a truly inspirational decade include Martin Sharp's covers for *Oz*, a satirical underground magazine with its roots in Sydney before being moved to London in 1966, and his poster for Bob Dylan the following year. Another Dylan poster, created the other side of the Atlantic by Milton Glaser in 1996, captures his hair as a pattern of psychedelic swirls. Robert Crumb's 'Fritz the Cat' cartoons, Michael English's poster for Jimi Hendrix, Victor Moscoso's covers for *Zap Comix* and Rick Griffin's sleeves for The Grateful Dead all lent a graphic edge to the decade and are remembered by those that grew up then, reinforcing the gap between the pre-war and post-war generations.

As the 1960s faded away and the 1970s emerged as the decade that taste forgot, a new graphic sensibility began to take shape. Influenced by the drugs that had engulfed the hippy years of the late 1960s, work took on the visual aesthetics of fantasy and science fiction in the illustrations by Roger Dean and Peter Jones. With the Hipgnosis sleeve for Pink Floyd's *Dark Side of the Moon*, the surreal photomontage of Tadanori Yokoo's sleeve for the Miles Davis album *Agharta* and Ian Beck's cover for Elton John's *Goodbye Yellow Brick Road*, the early to mid-1970s were a minefield of graphic languages.

It was the hard-edged sound of the street, and punk later in the decade, that influenced some notable changes to the visual landscape. With a new urban, gritty energetic sound came a raw, tougher approach to design with the 'cut and paste' graphic work for bands such as the Sex Pistols and The Clash. As punk and new wave adopted harder illustrative styles, designers like Barney Bubbles and his work for Elvis Costello, Ian Dury and The Damned, and Russell Mills with his projects for Penetration and Roger Eno, demonstrated a disregard for all that had come before.

Throughout the 1980s and 1990s, illustration's popularity rose and fell in equal measure. Memorable images by Ian Pollock for the National Theatre's production of King Lear vie alongside Pierre Le-Tan's masterly crafted covers for the *New Yorker*, whilst Brad Holland's atmospheric painted illustrations for numerous magazines, compete with work for Glynn Boyd Harte, Chloe Cheese, Dan Fern, Seymour Chwast, Paul Hogarth, Peter Till, George Hardie, Bush Holyhead, Graham Rawle and Brian Grimwood. Perhaps best known for their work spanning these decades are Gerald Scarfe for Pink Floyd's *The Wall* and Ralph Steadman's images for *Fear and Loathing in Las Vegas* by Hunter S. Thompson. The 1980s were a prolific time and despite cooling down in the 1990s as the last days of an analogue discipline gave way to a rebirth, rejuvenated by the possibilities of the digital, illustration continued to capture the moment.

So, what of life as an illustrator in the twenty-first century? Why the huge interest in following a career that can take years to break into, only to fizzle out in an instant? Why endure the possible rejection of a negative portfolio review or the aggravation of chasing an accounts department hell-bent on ignoring requests for payment months after an invoice was first overdue? It has more to do with the desire to communicate, to create images and see that work in print. The rush of opening a magazine to see your own work, witnessing people reading a book on the tube or subway that you created the cover illustration for, or passing a billboard ad campaign with your drawing on is truly undeniable.

Getting ahead in illustration takes commitment, personality and talent. It is unlikely that an illustrator lacking in any one of these areas will pick up commissions and, toughest of all, still be working in five years' time. Developing a personal visual language, getting to grips with materials and understanding the ins and outs of the industry is only part of the story. To succeed, you'll need some insider info – and you're holding it in your hands.

14

Chapter 1 — The illustrator as artist

When it comes to boundaries and borderlines, it is clear that illustration sits somewhere between art and design. Never truly considered to be an adjunct of art, nor wholly recognized as a solo design discipline, illustration has always awkwardly straddled the worlds of both artists and designers. Here, we look at some of the routes into illustration and some of the delights that life as an illustrator holds.

Illustration as a discipline

As we saw on pages 12–13, illustration has enjoyed a long and varied history, spanning many applications, from book covers to title sequences. But its tendency to cross disciplines has also been its misfortune. Outside of education, there appears to have been a tendency for artists to ignore the importance of the role that illustration plays in their discipline. The crossover from art to illustration is occasionally deemed appropriate, but the reverse is rarely accepted. In the design world, designers plunder freely from the fields of illustration, yet rarely take any responsibility for sowing new seeds, and little time or space is given to nurturing growth and emerging talent.

Back in education, the discipline has fared little better; the number of institutions offering full-time courses purely in illustration is only just beginning to rise significantly. Those that do, however, offer little by way of stand-alone facilities. Illustration courses often do not occupy their own physical space, but sit in studios as part of graphic design courses. It is still the case that in many countries across Europe, illustration has failed to be recognized as a discipline and therefore courses tend not to exist at all. Professionally, illustrations for press and advertising have been created by designers and artists, and with no real recognition for the practice, the development of courses has remained as an off-shoot of graphic design, if at all.

Of course it is true that crossover and discussion can be nurtured across the two disciplines of graphic design and illustration. But this is only possible if both are given equal status. With a high demand for facilities and studio space for courses requiring specialist equipment such as looms in textiles, kilns in ceramics, wood, metal and plastics workshops in 3D design and black-and-white and digital darkrooms in photography, it is clear – although unjustified – why illustration often remains at the end of the list.

New directions

Despite all this, however, with the relatively recent growth of online blogs, websites and digital media, and thanks in part to the increasing popularity of new media such as video games, graffiti art and graphic novels, illustration is finally becoming a better recognized discipline. New territories and opportunities for self-promotion mean that the value, popularity and profitability of this evolving and expanding applied art form is gradually allowing it to assert itself as a subject in its own right.

'Outside of education, there appears to have been a tendency for artists to ignore the importance of the role that illustration plays in their discipline.'

1.1
City painting.
Ben Kelly
This painting, worked up from initial sketchbook drawings, was developed for an exhibition of the illustrator as artist. It is only relatively recently that illustrators have started to be taken seriously as artists in their own right.

1. The illustrator as artist   2. The medium is the message   3. From outcomes to outlets   4. Communicating ideas   5. Making it happen   6. Production

Illustration as a discipline   The new wave of illustrators →

1.1

The new wave of illustrators

Much of the recent resurgence of interest in illustration owes its success to a power shift that happened in the early 2000s. Interestingly, a revolution was taking place away from the confines of professional illustration and the often-stifling demands of commercial work. The uprising was subtle and not started on the battlegrounds familiar to the old guard of illustrators. A new wave was honing its skills away from regular illustration outlets, producing work that refused to pander to the art directors of glossy monthly magazines or the Sunday supplements.

The new wave of illustrators with a new approach, with something to say and the ways and means of saying it, started to command control. No longer indulging the needs of dull business-to-business corporate clients, a savvier, more fashion-conscious, streetwise illustrator had started to create images for an audience made up of its own peers. Independent magazines and record labels, the established 'style' press, as well as small fashion companies started to employ the services of this new breed.

Key moments

The following two moments are now recognized as key in the rebirth of illustration. In the UK, *The Face* magazine employed an illustrator as art director and the look and feel of the magazine changed almost overnight. Funky, quirky and urban images by new illustrators started to appear and the ratio of illustration to photography was healthier than ever before. In the US, Levi's were quick to capture the new mood and commissioned illustrators to create ad campaigns and illustrate their urban clothing ranges, breaking the mould and allowing illustration to depict fashion in a way that had been the proviso of the photographer. Keen to capture the zeitgeist and stay ahead of the pack, this new and increasing client list took to 'new' illustration with open arms. But what had really changed within illustration?

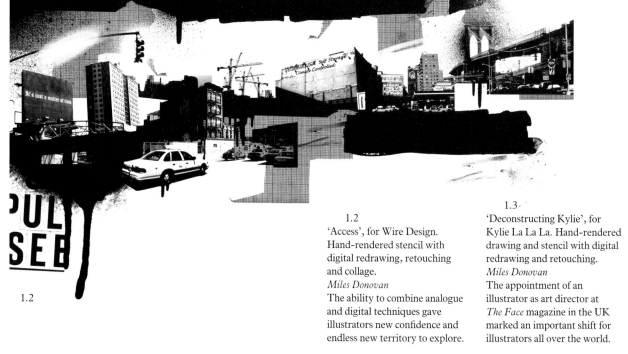

1.2

1.2
'Access', for Wire Design. Hand-rendered stencil with digital redrawing, retouching and collage.
Miles Donovan
The ability to combine analogue and digital techniques gave illustrators new confidence and endless new territory to explore.

1.3
'Deconstructing Kylie', for Kylie La La La. Hand-rendered drawing and stencil with digital redrawing and retouching.
Miles Donovan
The appointment of an illustrator as art director at *The Face* magazine in the UK marked an important shift for illustrators all over the world.

THE FACE

ED FASHION

eastie Boys

Manic Street Preachers

Christopher Walken

KYLIE

WHO'S THAT GIRL?

9 770263 121026   06>

INTERNATIONAL MAGAZINE OF THE YEAR

1.3

Catalysts for change

The revolution had occurred for a number of reasons; the first was the average age of the new image-maker. Younger but already with an established grip on taming the technology, this new breed felt empowered rather than hindered. Not being tied down by the baggage of time, nor attempting to pacify the old guard or fit into an existing order, allowed the renegades of 'new' illustration the freedom to experiment.

Another reason for change stemmed from what really excited these fresh illustrators; the scope now offered by the mix of digital and analogue techniques. Introduced to a vast range of techniques and media during their first foundation course at art school and able to refine their skills throughout the nomadic existence that typified degree-level teaching of illustration, an enthusiasm had grown for what they considered 'new' technology; traditional techniques and methods. The eclectic nature of their image-making skills was to be matched only by the eclectic nature of the subjects and themes covered and explored by these new illustrators.

The themes explored by this new wave were not new – many of them are already well-investigated and documented within editorial and fine art photography – but for illustration it was a much-needed shot in the arm.

'Not being tied down by the baggage of time, nor attempting to pacify the old guard or fit into an existing order, allowed the renegades of "new" illustration the freedom to experiment.'

1.4 and 1.5
'Cornershopcornucopiarama'
for Marmalade magazine.
Digital vector drawing and
'These Arms', for Oxfam.
Digital vector drawing.
Mr Bingo
Much of the subject matter
being tackled by this new
breed of illustrator offered
opportunities to create work
of a humorous and playful
nature, as well as hard-hitting
campaigns of a graphic nature.

1.4

1. The illustrator as artist   2. The medium is the message   3. From outcomes to outlets   4. Communicating ideas   5. Making it happen   6. Production

← Illustration as a discipline   The new wave of illustrators   Art school ethos →

Art school ethos

From that first life-drawing class in the studio to the induction session in the print-making workshop or the introductory class in the darkroom, it is clear that art school offers a wealth of new creative opportunities to the young artist or designer. Generally it is recognized in art and design education that students will study a one-year basic course in art and design before embarking upon a more specialized three-year programme in their chosen field. In the UK and Europe this general foundation course has often sat outside of the degree programme, but recently there has been an enthusiasm to adopt the model used in the USA, where the first year of art and design education is subsumed into the degree, effectively offering a four-year programme. Maintaining the flavour of the foundation course will be important as this happens, as it is here that students are first introduced to new ways of working and thinking.

Mixing interests

The initial foundation year of study allows students to briefly experience numerous disciplines within the broad spread of art and design. This can then be used to help choose what to study at degree level. During this time, students may be studying alongside those that have chosen to practice architecture, fashion, ceramics or automotive design for example, and it is in this mix of interests that many find inspiration for their work. Perhaps as important as the opportunity for practice, a strong art and design foundation course offers study, reflection and debate on art and design history, communication theories, politics and issues of race and gender.

This vital year of study, will, for many, be the only real opportunity for students from a variety of disciplines to discuss and debate issues. As students migrate towards their more subject-specific courses in the following year, they inevitably find themselves surrounded by others with similar interests and goals. For creative young artists and designers this can stifle debate and create unnecessary boundaries between disciplines that may never again be broken down. It is the division of disciplines and the creation of walled subject areas that helps to stamp out new, forward-thinking and possibly radical approaches to practice. Of course, questions will still be asked and debate will continue to rage, but only from within each of the divided subjects, and without external opinions and contributions much can remain unaltered and unchallenged.

1.6
'Garbage Heads'. Marker pen and paint on metal construction.
Akira Wakui
Working from small-scale original drawings made with ink on paper, these larger metal constructions are hand-crafted before being hand-painted with drawn elements added prior to installation within a gallery environment.

1.6

22

A demanding life

Illustration is not for the faint-hearted. It can take a tough cookie to meet the demands and rigours of getting somewhere within a discipline that feels vastly undersupported. Without stand alone facilities in education, the lone illustrator must utilize the media that other disciplines would first lay claim to, breaking into places that would normally be considered the domain of other specialists. Gaining access to the drawing studio normally housed in the fine art department, the darkrooms occupied by the photography course, the print-making workshops open for students of print-making, the wood and metal workshops utilized by students of sculpture, architecture and furniture design and the computing facilities overrun by graphic design and motion graphics students is never going to be easy. But it happens – illustration students are a rare breed that open doors and get things moving.

The drive to create images

A life without a defined career path is not for all: creating and then maintaining a presence as an illustrator within the design industry takes commitment and can at times be frustrating. Dragging a portfolio of work to a potential client to find that they have left the building is depressing, and being at the mercy of those with the power to commission can be demoralizing, but at the heart of those that wish to work in illustration is the desire to create images.

Working with new materials, solving visual problems, researching subjects and experimenting with ideas, all drive most illustrators. Seen by many as a lifestyle rather than just a career choice, the commitment to the discipline must be all-encompassing if a student illustrator is to break into the commercial world. Never likely to be a regular nine-to-five existence with healthcare, dental and paid holidays, illustration demands total involvement. Working across the board, breaking across boundaries, experimenting and mastering media, none truly belonging to them, the illustrator still finds ways of making his or her mark.

1.7
Crisis illustrations for a poster campaign, album cover and other promotional materials for the charity single, 'Crisis Consequences'.
Mia Nilsson
Based on the game 'Consequences', a group of artists including Beth Ditto, Paul Weller and Pearl Lowe got together to create a charity single. Mia Nilsson's illustration and Stefi Orazi's designs were used to promote the single.

1.7

1. The illustrator as artist   2. The medium is the message   3. From outcomes to outlets   4. Communicating ideas   5. Making it happen   6. Production

← Art school ethos   A demanding life   Case study: John Clementson →

Case study: John Clementson

This artwork forms a spread from the Michael Rosen book *Crow and Hawk,* which re-tells a traditional Pueblo tale from New Mexico. The story looks at themes of responsibility, using three main characters: Crow, Hawk and Eagle.

The commission

John initially produced a book plan and sample spread, which were taken to the Bologna and Frankfurt book fairs. Both books were 'picked-up' by Harcourt Brace in the USA.

John had a lot of control over the layout of the work, and Jackie Fortey, the Art Director, was happy for the work to progress in this way. Jackie had considerably more experience in this field than John and was a great help with the project.

John had to allow space for foreign-language translations, so he produced panels for the typography containing decorative elements that could be removed.

Initial response

Initial roughs were produced on loose sheets of paper and John then made a selection and cleaned them up for presentation. The artworks were made using Pantone Uncoated Paper and were spray-mounted onto Arches or Fabriano hot-press paper.

Final artwork

The spread shown here looks at the selfless efforts of Hawk to ensure the hatching of Crow's eggs while Crow is off out having a good time. The illustration cleverly conveys the passing of time and the patience and stoic devotion of Hawk.

1.8

1. The illustrator as artist   2. The medium is the message   3. From outcomes to outlets   4. Communicating ideas   5. Making it happen   6. Production

← A demanding life   Case study: John Clementson   Try it yourself... →

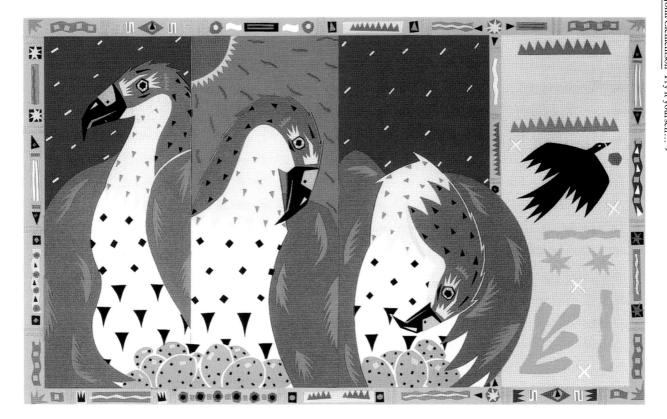

1.8
Rough designs and final
illustration for *Crow and Hawk*.
John Clementson
On projects such as these, the
role of illustrator can strongly
determine the final outcome.

Try it yourself…

The illustrator as artist

Allowing yourself to experiment with ideas that are generated by you, rather than a given brief, is essential for your own personal development.

Materials

Experiment with new materials or include collage in your work. If you tend to use wet media such as ink or watercolour then opt for charcoal or pastels. You should vary the scale that you work to, if you tend to work small, work on a large scale, and vice versa.

The brief: Initiating ideas

Create a piece of work based on a memory. This will mean that your subject and content is very personal and can only be directed by you. Try scanning in old documents or fabric within your image. Focus on one memory from your own life and develop ideas through to a finished piece.

Questions in summary

1. Which other disciplines might an illustrator borrow from or lend to?
2. How has illustration developed as a subject since its earliest beginnings?
3. Why has illustration found it hard to distinguish itself as a subject in its own right?

1. The illustrator as artist   2. The medium is the message   3. From outcomes to outlets   4. Communicating ideas   5. Making it happen   6. Production

← Try it yourself…   Questions in summary

Chapter 2 — The medium is the message

Illustrators communicate solely through their work; their subject matter and the strength of their ideas are vital aspects of the job. Less obvious, but as crucial, is the choice of medium. When answering a brief, getting the choice of materials right is just as important as getting the concept right.

The power of the pencil

A common belief amongst graphic designers is that because the power of typography is entrusted to them alone, they hold all of the cards in the game of commercial design for print and screen. A little-known, or perhaps just rarely commented-upon fact that matches or even surpasses the claim to type by the designer, is that the illustrator commands the power of the pencil. The pencil, and with it the activity of drawing in its broadest sense, is what defines the practice of illustration today.

2.1
'Down the well'. Pencil drawings in an old novel.
Matt Jones
The simplest, yet least forgiving media is pencil. There is very little room for error – an illustration rests on the artist's skills and ability.

2.2
'The Broken Column'. Pencil drawing made for the magazine *Fashion Tale*.
Annelie Carlström
(Stylist: Kattis Lindoff)
Photoshop may be used to clean and tidy up an image, but strong drawing techniques are the essence of the image.

Drawing and 'image-making'

It is hard to believe, but drawing can be a controversial subject. From the start of the journey from school pupil to art student and on to fully paid-up member of the illustration community, the practice of drawing can cause heated debate amongst practitioners. Art school teaching may seem radically different to students from the way in which they had been 'taught' previously. The use of new terminology also reflects a new stance and approach to this complex subject that may feel alien at first. The new vocabulary introduces phrases such as 'interpretative mark marking', 'intuitive and observational drawing of the figure', and 'exploring negative space'. For the first time, students may be encouraged to 'work back into a drawing with charcoal'. The essence of this approach to 'image-making' is to encourage experimentation, rather than just training students in observational skills. This approach has typified the teaching of the subject since the 1950s and '60s.

2.2

1. The illustrator as artist 2. The medium is the message 3. From outcomes to outlets 4. Communicating ideas 5. Making it happen 6. Production

The power of the pencil Material world →

Ways of drawing

The teaching of drawing will vary from art school to art school and may be influenced by fashions and movements in art and design. Although it might appear that artists and illustrators both approach the discipline from similar positions, the reality is somewhat different. Opinions are divided on the purpose of practice.

Generally, however, artists work to a self-set agenda, whilst illustrators start from a client-written brief. The artist may create work as part of the journey to the final solution, whilst the illustrator will produce work that ultimately sits within another context; that of the printed magazine or book jacket, reproduced from the original.

Drawing can be used for recording, representing and portraying. It can be observational or interpretative, can reflect a mood or a moment, or be utilized purely to convey information. Drawing is a hugely broad discipline and in the context of illustration, in the hands of illustrators, it is pushed to its very limits.

2.3
'Vandal' for Nike. Biro on paper.
Billie-Jean
Different forms of drawing bring a certain substance to a project – the use of the ballpoint pen on lined paper evokes memories of doodling in school exercise books.

2.3

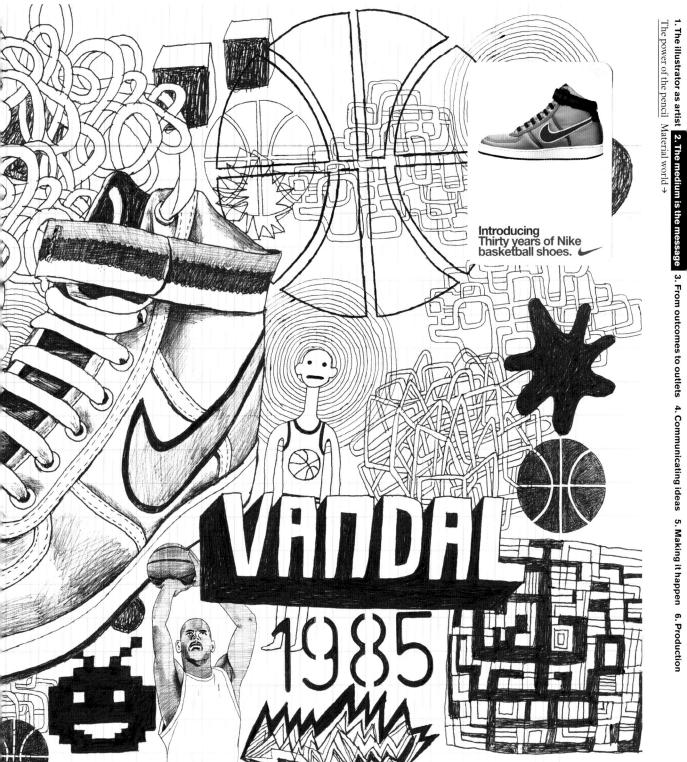

Introducing
Thirty years of Nike
basketball shoes. ✓Nike

VANDAL
1985

1. The illustrator as artist   2. The medium is the message   3. From outcomes to outlets   4. Communicating ideas   5. Making it happen   6. Production

The power of the pencil   Material world →

2.4

34

Material world

The job of the illustrator is relatively simple; the key to successful illustrating is in the essence of the message and the art of communication. It is, however, the medium or materials employed to convey that message that can assist in the correct reading and understanding. A strong idea visually translated using the most appropriate media, with excellent execution, will always lead to the most successful illustrative solutions.

Choosing materials

With the apparent freedom of choice in medium, comes a responsibility and understanding for their historical or cultural nature, and the context in which they are to be applied. There is little to be gained from illustrating mobile phone technology, for example, using an etching process. Working in a very linear way only in a vector application for an article about street market vendors would not demonstrate an affinity for the subject; the themes and messages would be distorted, and the medium might act as a barrier to the understanding of the message.

Equally, acknowledging historical and subject-specific references to materials ensures messages cannot be confused; why work in the flat, bold, primary-coloured comic style reminiscent of Roy Lichtenstein's Pop Art for an illustration about the global stock markets? The perfect marriage of materials and message may sound like a cliché but makes real sense; after all, the mantra that 'form follows function' still holds a resonance today.

At the heart of all illustration, drawing plays a vital role. Without the ability to draw and visualize well, the illustrator lacks the most important component in his or her toolbox. Illustrators have at their fingertips, literally in this digital age, tools that enable the creation of complex, layered, multifaceted images that can be created using a multitude of techniques. But without the power of the pencil, the illustrator may be as powerless as the designer that has failed to control typography.

1. The illustrator as artist
← The power of the pencil | Material world
2. The medium is the message
Material world   The use of odd media →
3. From outcomes to outlets   4. Communicating ideas   5. Making it happen   6. Production

AUTHOR TIP:
FINDING YOUR OWN WAY OF WORKING

— Methods of working can take many years to fine-tune and make unique to an individual illustrator.
— There is always a temptation to take creative short-cuts – it's better to invest the time and effort in creating a way of working that no-one else is doing, though.
— Finding materials and processes that 'click' is part of the journey that all illustrators must take in order to create truly unique images.
— Increasingly, illustrators are employing a range of methods and techniques that cross the divide between analogue and digital worlds.

2.4
'Bear and Hunter'. Digital drawings.
Adrian Johnson
Even when based on pencil drawings or original layouts created in sketchbooks, work that uses digital elements – be that anything from vector lines or scanned textures – is still classified as being done entirely on-screen.

Celebrating process

The process of creating images is a complex and personal journey for every individual illustrator. Often, seemingly simple images can belie both the craft of the image-maker and the journey that the illustrator may have taken over previous years in order to reach a point where creating work becomes second nature. Graduates of illustration courses often expect an instant flow of commissions, but it can take numerous months and occasionally years of honing and fine-tuning work before an image-maker feels truly confident as an illustrator.

Much of the struggle towards professionalism can be about the materials and processes that the illustrator starts to excel in working with; understanding how to use particular media can take time and practice, but is vital in mastering the ability to illustrate effectively and therefore professionally.

Many illustrators have a favourite range of materials that they will choose to work with. For many, the blend and scope of their chosen materials, tools and techniques is what helps to define the work that they produce. Experimenting with techniques and ways of working can be more important than exploring the scope of drawing and image-making itself. There are illustrators that work using the most simple methods imaginable – using a pencil, pen or paintbrush mark – whilst there are others that build up complex layers utilizing techniques in photography, vector-applications and scanned montages of 'found' imagery, often priding themselves on their ability to hide the processes from the viewer. It is the celebration of the process and the techniques employed that interest and drive this particular breed of illustrators.

2.5

2.5
Untitled. Multiple techniques.
Blair Frame
Multiple techniques have been used here to retain a hand-made quality.

2.6
'Metamorphosis'. Collage, paint and digital processes.
Maria Forrester
Many illustrators find that they have a favourite range of materials to work with.

1. The illustrator as artist   **2. The medium is the message**   3. From outcomes to outlets   4. Communicating ideas   5. Making it happen   6. Production

← The power of the pencil   Material world   The use of odd media →

2.6

The use of odd media

Using paint straight out of the tube is frowned upon by the serious artist who feels it is important to mix the desired colour oneself rather than relying on the manufacturer to create the very hue needed. This may sound pompous or exaggerated, but the importance of the right materials for the artist should never be underestimated.

For some, the allure of the art store and its contents is never enough and the route to creating truly original art is in re-appropriating existing or 'found' objects. Some illustrators create images from collaged elements, mixing and layering in both analogue and digital formats to create new variants.

Collage is not a new art form, it originally came to prominence with the birth of photography, but appears to have been given a new lease of life by digital technology. Originally created by graphic designers, the first to master the Mac in the late 1980s, collaged illustrations were created in applications such as Adobe Photoshop. Within a few years the illustrator had gained on lost ground and the range of illustrative expertise in the field of collage began to expand.

Making pictures from more challenging materials has interested illustrators wanting to ensure that their work is considered original. Using cut and torn coloured paper in the style of Henri Matisse, or creating 'Box Art' in the manner of Joseph Cornell has attracted some illustrators away from traditional techniques, whilst others strive to use objects and items previously unused as art materials.

Illustrations created from coloured push pins set into a squared grid, or from cut and painted sheets of tin, or entirely collaged from tiny slivers of banknotes have all appeared in publications. The range of experimentation and sophistication employed across these untried and untested applications sets illustrators apart from others in the design profession; if a material has artistic potential, there is an illustrator ready to master it.

2.8
'Samuel Beckett'. Drilled holes in MDF board.
Will Tomlinson
Creating an image using light and shade by drilling holes of differing depths according to a pre-set pattern gives a new vision to the photographic portrait of Samuel Beckett. Although this image appears to have used digital processes at the end of its creation, in measuring the holes, this wasn't the case. A photo of Beckett was just digitally scanned at the beginning and reduced to just a few monochrome tones in Photoshop.

2.7
'Shine like a Star'.
Hand-cut paper.
Pinky
Building layers of colour utilizing a similar method to the way in which a screenprint is created, but using hand-cut coloured papers allows detail to show through in a unique and varied way.

2.7

1. The illustrator as artist 2. The medium is the message 3. From outcomes to outlets 4. Communicating ideas 5. Making it happen 6. Production

← Material world   The use of odd media   Using photography →

2.8

Using photography

'Carry a camera with you at all times' has long been the advice to budding photographers by hardened commercial pros, specialists and teaching staff. Now, recording life with a camera has become the norm for practitioners of all art and design disciplines as well as photographers.

Illustrators have used photography as a reference tool for many years. For those who create drawings on location, the camera has provided an excellent memory-jogger. Many will aim to record as much information as possible on-site and then return to the studio to complete the work from the photographic reference. The final artwork may show no real evidence of the photo, but behind the scenes it has nevertheless played a part. Perhaps a more obvious use of photography for illustrators has been in the recent upsurge in the popularity of vector applications to 'trace' photographs, rather than relying on pure drawing skills. Quite simply, a photographic image, often reduced to either line or high contrast black and white in Adobe Photoshop, is placed on to a fresh layer in an application such as Adobe Illustrator.

Using drawing tools, normally with a range of different widths and finishes, a drawing is created by tracing over the photo in the original layer onto a new one. Some vector applications now also offer an 'auto-trace' feature that can take some of the work out of the tracing.

A more obvious use of photography within illustration has been in the use of collage and photomontage. Prior to possible digital solutions this would have meant the reproduction and printing of a photographic image that might then be trimmed or cut out and glued into place within another image. Often collage artists utilize a range of 'found' materials that may also include collected ephemera, as well as photographic images. Artists that work in photomontage may choose to set up models and situations, as a true photographer might, in order to create the desired effect. Elements are then often cut and pasted into new positions within other images. The availability of digital manipulation has ensured that this entire process is somewhat smoother, even allowing the artist to download photographic images for use in work from online image banks. With most mobile phones now also featuring cameras, the advice about taking a camera everywhere might finally sound a little too obvious.

2.9
'Clowns – DIY', for FAD.
Constructed photographic montage.
Chrissie Macdonald
Photography has long been a perfect medium for the illustrator. Used by many as a reference tool, capturing images that are recreated back in the studio or used directly in the image-making process.

AUTHOR TIP:
WORKING WITH PHOTOGRAPHERS

— Seek the advice and skills of a friendly, professional photographer or studio if possible – they know all the tricks of the trade and may even lend you the right kit.
— Use the best digital camera you can afford or borrow and ensure that it is on the highest quality setting.
— Use a tripod – these are inexpensive and will ensure that camera shake does not ruin your shots.
— Make sure that you either use natural light, if available, or tungsten bulbs in your lighting. Be aware of any shadows.
— Test your shots before you take too many. Take the first few photos to your Mac or PC and check that they are of a high enough resolution and that the lighting is correct.

1. The illustrator as artist 2. The medium is the message 3. From outcomes to outlets 4. Communicating ideas 5. Making it happen 6. Production

← The use of odd media Using photography Mixing media →

2.9

Mixing media

Without the confines of a discipline-specific medium, the illustrator has been free to explore and experiment with a range of media, creating images from whatever and wherever seems most appropriate. With drawing at the centre of the illustrator's armoury, the handmade mark is never far from view, but unsurprisingly it is the vast range of potential image and mark-making devices that appears in the work of, and typifies the eclectic nature of, today's image-makers.

Like professional magpies, illustrators plunder an array of media, mixing and matching working methods depending on the requirements of the project. It is not uncommon to witness a raw visual mix of the digital, the analogue, the traditional, the photographic and the stencilled, as well as hand-drawn and painted marks within the images of contemporary illustrators. The digital has empowered the illustrator in a way that was unthinkable even just a decade and a half ago.

'It is not uncommon to witness a raw visual mix of the digital, the analogue, the traditional, the photographic and the stencilled, as well as hand-drawn and painted marks within the images of contemporary illustrators.'

2.10

1. The illustrator as artist 2. The medium is the message 3. From outcomes to outlets 4. Communicating ideas 5. Making it happen 6. Production

← Using photography Mixing media Using the computer →

2.10
'Monkey Dust' for the BBC. Digital drawing and digital photographic composite.
2.11
'Stairs', for the NHS. Digital drawing and digital photographic composite.
Andrew Rae
Combining hand-rendered, digitally drawn characters with real, digitally shot backgrounds, gives an image a realistic yet edgy feel. Equally effective can be the dropping in of a photographic sky to a hand-drawn and coloured illustration.

2.11

Using the computer

No one tool or process has had as much influence on the methods employed by the illustrator as the computer. If it is the pencil that wields the power, then it is the computer that harnesses that power and enables the illustrator to transform the pencil mark into a seemingly never-ending array of new marks. The rebirth and revival of interest in the craft of illustration can be attributed directly to the role that the computer has played.

The computer has opened illustration up to a full range of digital possibilities and placed it on a level with other disciplines. The technical power now found within the reach of most illustrators – has ensured a more equal relationship with design. Illustrators, with the aid of digital processes, are returning to the roots of the practice. Illustration first grew from a branch of graphic design that was commercial art, and now increased involvement with projects and commissions during the design stage has begun to echo that early approach as illustrators increasingly work across the board.

Creating artwork that was 'camera ready' became the only technical requirement for illustrators in the years leading to the digital revolution; as many were working less in design studios and more and more from their own studios and homes, it was easy for illustrators to be left out of the loop when it came to making design decisions about projects. Digital technology started to change the input that illustrators would have, allowing opportunities for discussion and debate about reproduction issues, print processes and paper stocks, as well as entirely digital outlets for illustration such as the Web and television. Contributing to these changes in practice were both the power and knowledge digital illustrators now had access to and the ease of communication afforded by email and mobile phone technology. From their own freelance workspace illustrators could work alongside designers with communication lines open at all times.

A relationship built on trust began to evolve slowly as illustrators started to emerge from the dawn of their own digital age – albeit ten years after the desk-top revolution had re-energized graphic design – with portfolios of work that impressed a younger more streetwise design community. Constantly looking for new ways of expressing ideas and communicating to their clients, graphic design saw a fresh approach to image-making in digital illustration. Impressed with the ability to harness both absolute skills in drawing and image manipulation alongside the vast array of possibilities that digitalization opened up, graphic design began to recognize the importance of illustration within the design process.

'...it is the computer that harnesses that power and enables the illustrator to transform the pencil mark into a seemingly never-ending array of new marks.'

Digital timeline

1971	The floppy disk arrives from IBM
1972	Computer games begin to appear, with 'Pong' for the Atari
1975	Bill Gates starts Microsoft
1976	Steve Jobs and Steve Wozniak start Apple Computer
1978	First computer-generated film title appears, in *Superman*
1984	Universal studios opens Computer Generation (CG) department; the first Macintosh computer is sold
1985	Windows appears for the first time
1987	Adobe launch Illustrator
1989	Adobe launch Photoshop
1994	The WWW revolution gets fully underway as the number of hosts hits two million; Pixar produces Toy Story; MP3 is developed and accepted as the standard compression platform for storing music digitally
1997	DVD technology announced and within a few years can be played and recorded on personal computers
2000	San Francisco Museum of Modern Art launches 'Playstation 2 010101 – Art in Technological Times' exhibition
2001	Apple launch a range of G4 Powerbooks
2003	Adobe launch Creative Suite, a professional integrated software package comprising of Photoshop, Illustrator and InDesign
2004	Social networking site Facebook is launched
2005	E-commerce website Etsy is launched, allowing users to buy and sell handmade or vintage items, as well as art and craft supplies
2006	*Time* magazine name their 2006 person of the year as 'You', following the meteoric rise of the blog and other user-generated content
2008	Twitter's engineering team make architectural changes to the site in order to cope with growing demand; Apple opens its app store, offering software applications for iPhone
2010	Steve Jobs launches Apple iPad

1. The illustrator as artist 2. The medium is the message 3. From outcomes to outlets 4. Communicating ideas 5. Making it happen 6. Production

← Mixing media Using the computer Case study: Tim Vyner →

Computers and the future of illustration

The digital age has opened so many new doors for illustration. Only time will tell how this will be taken forward by new generations of illustrators. For many though, questions remain about just how safe the work of the illustrator is. As with most things in life, with new opportunities come new risks. Will the increasing prevalence of online management and stock libraries erode the rights of creatives, for example? Will illustration be replaced by animation? Will the rise of illustrative collectives reduce the potential for individuality? These are all questions that the forward-thinking illustrator must consider.

Recent shifts in the book and music publishing industries threaten the existence of traditional book and CD/ record art. Many commissions now go way above and beyond the typical ad or book cover. On the other hand, the rise of online social media and new technology that allows integration of illustration, photography and film, has created more opportunities for creatives. The predominance of digital production means that output is faster and combinations with other art forms are simpler. It is essential for the illustrator to adapt to the changes that these seismic shifts in the commercial art world will bring.

Key to this will be the art of self-promotion. As creatives vie for attention in our increasingly crowded online spaces, the need to stand out is stronger than ever. It is more than likely that this quest for individuality will be what really drives illustration forward in years to come.

2.12

'…the rise of online social media and new technology that allows integration of illustration, photography and film, has created more opportunities for creatives.'

2.12
'We Have Always lived in the Castle'.
Computer-aided poster design.
Tom Duxbury
Although drawing by hand can be incredibly rewarding, using the computer can launch work into a fast-paced environment where illustrators can make sense of the exciting but complex interplay between shape, layout and colour.

1. The illustrator as artist 2. The medium is the message 3. From outcomes to outlets 4. Communicating ideas 5. Making it happen 6. Production

← Mixing media Using the computer Case study: Tim Vyner →

Case study: Tim Vyner

Tim Vyner is a reportage artist, illustrator and educator. He has recorded many global sporting events over the last decade including FIFA World Cups, European Championships, and Olympic Games. His work is held in many collections and is published in magazines and books in the UK, where he is based, and internationally.

2.13

The commission

Sports business partners funded Tim to travel to China to record and document the atmosphere and experience of the Beijing Olympic Games. He was asked to capture an extraordinary moment in the city's history when the whole world would be watching.

Initial response

Tim used a sketchbook to record figures, events and specific moments, and a camera to record architectural details. This allowed Tim to capture the atmosphere of Beijing at a specific moment in time.

Access

Approval was required for access to specific areas of the Olympic Park, so Tim was only able to explore and record the areas that his ticket gave him access to.

2.13
Beijing street scenes.
Tim Vyner
Tim Vyner was commissioned to record the atmosphere and experience of the Beijing Olympic Games.

1. The illustrator as artist   2. The medium is the message   3. From outcomes to outlets   4. Communicating ideas   5. Making it happen   6. Production

← Using the computer   Case study: Tim Vyner   Try it yourself… →

Case study: Tim Vyner

Final artwork

A series of reportage drawings and large scale watercolour paintings were produced for exhibition and publication.

Completion

Tim's work was eventually published and exhibited. More than 80 of his images were exhibited at the Bankside Gallery in London, UK. The exhibition deadline was a useful end point to work towards. Exhibiting work is often where the illustrator feels most exposed and knowing he had to fill a gallery, which would be attended by many Olympic athletes, organizers and representatives spurred Tim on to a conclusion.

2.14
Birds Nest, Beijing.
Tim Vyner
Tim used his sketchbook to record figures, events and specific moments but used a camera to record architectural details which he could then later work into his watercolour pieces.

2.14

1. The illustrator as artist | **2. The medium is the message** | 3. From outcomes to outlets | 4. Communicating ideas | 5. Making it happen | 6. Production

← Using the computer | Case study: Tim Vyner | Try it yourself... →

Try it yourself…

The medium is the message

Illustrators tend to find a way of working that suits them and then stick to this as their personal style. But the new ideas that experimenting with new methods and materials can bring should never be underestimated.

Materials

You will need some glue or tape, scissors, paper as a base for the drawings, sugar paper, newspaper, found tickets, old gift-wrap, foil, wrappers – anything that can be cut up for the purposes of creating a drawing.

The brief: Mixing media

Drawing is essential for illustration but this does not mean that drawing always has to be undertaken in the conventional sense. Try 'drawing' with paper, found objects and ephemera. Place one or two items on a table and 'draw' them using only cut out pieces from the materials you have gathered.

Don't use any pencil, pen, paint or hand-directed media – this is about looking at the objects in front of you and reforming them in a different media.

You could also try 'drawing' with modelling clay.

Questions in summary

1. How do we define drawing? How do these definitions differ from 'drawing' in its traditional sense and 'drawing' in an image-making sense?
2. How can the illustrator incorporate more unusual materials in their work?
3. How have digital materials changed illustration and how are they likely to change for the future?

Chapter 3 — From outcomes to outlets

It is one thing to master the art of illustration from the comfort of the art school studio or the warmth of the back bedroom, but working to commission, faced with a real brief, a real client and a real deadline is an entirely different process. Different sectors of the design, advertising and publishing worlds each have their own complexities and demands.

3.1

The overview

The illustrator's business landscape of design, advertising and publishing has undergone enormous change during the past few decades. The role that graphic communication plays in our everyday lives, here at the start of the twenty-first century, has never been more intense, complex and demanding for the viewer.

In this increasingly digital age, visual communication must compete fiercely for our attention, and we stand in the firing line. Free magazines are thrust at us as we leave railway stations, we are handed club flyers on every other urban street corner and we are broadcast to 24 hours a day, 365 days of the year, by a seemingly endless array of TV channels.

We are fired at by promos, advertorials and infomercials. We are spammed, texted and profiled. Visual communication is online, on-screen, downloadable and upgradable. Never before have we been so bombarded from every quarter, so image-saturated, manically marketed to and media-manipulated. And we only have ourselves to blame for this situation as the media feeds an insatiable thirst from a knowledge-hungry public: we ceaselessly demand the latest, the newest and the best, devouring information at a truly astonishing rate with no let-up from the avalanche that we have created.

To even compete in this cut-throat communication war, those companies that seek to differentiate their products and publications have started to understand that creating a brand awareness which offers a unique vision or visual can, in turn, offer some small measure of individualism in this crowded marketplace. Illustration has thus found favour once again, not just because interesting, sassy work is in evidence, but because it is the key to creating images that reflect more than just photographic evidence. Illustration has the power to capture a personality, a point of view. It can encapsulate a mood or a moment, and can tell a story to give a product history, depth and meaning.

The design studio

However powerful illustration as a form of communication is, without graphic design, it would struggle to exist. Graphic design communicates, persuades, informs and educates. It covers a vast array of commercial applications and in trying to visualize the scope and breadth of the discipline it is wise to remember that all communication design has emerged from its practice.

The street sign, the book or newspaper, the CD sleeve, the instructions on the medicine bottle, the pack that contains your favourite brand of breakfast cereal or the software that you use have all been touched by the hand of the graphic designer.

The design studio sits at the heart of commercial graphics and these companies, or departments of bigger organizations, work across the various diverse sectors of the industry.

The scope of work for design companies and studios can be endless and it is here that the working relationship with graphic design starts for the illustrator. Understanding how the industry operates and how the numerous sectors function is fundamental to ensuring that the relationship with graphic design can be most fruitfully exploited.

3.1
'Foreign Service'.
Ian Dodds
Day after day, we are bombarded with images and information that vies for our attention. In an increasingly visual world, it is illustration that holds the key to giving a small measure of individualism to the marketplace.

1. The illustrator as artist 2. The medium is the message **3. From outcomes to outlets** 4. Communicating ideas 5. Making it happen 6. Production

The overview Editorial illustration →

Editorial illustration

Editorial illustration is fundamental to most illustrators and is the bread-and-butter work for most professionals.

Using illustration makes real sense for the editor of a newspaper supplement or magazine. Where photography is used to present an image as fact, illustration can be applied to features to indicate a personal viewpoint or an idea. It is the contrast that illustration offers to photography that works so well in editorial projects and it is rare to find illustration used outside of this in a publishing context.

Due to massive increases in the number and circulation of digital and print newspapers and magazines, and the knock-on increase in feature or opinion-driven articles, there is a plethora of commissions available every month. Add to the stock available in most newsagents and book stores the huge number of in-house magazines produced for insurance companies, banks, airlines, retail outlets and others, and the number of potential commissions grows accordingly. Illustrators working successfully in this huge sector can keep themselves very busy.

In editorial illustration, budgets can be tight and it is important for the professional to maintain a steady flow of work and to ensure invoices are issued on a regular basis. Despite the relatively low fees, most illustrators still enjoy the creative freedom of working for newspapers and magazines; being left to be inventive and original are the rewards here. The freedom to develop new working methods within a project, showcase skills and test new ideas without excessive art direction from an art director or editor can be invaluable. For those illustrators given a regular 'slot' in a weekly or monthly magazine, the challenge of developing fresh ideas for the same subject on a regular basis can be enjoyably stimulating.

Art direction

Understanding how illustrators are commissioned is key to successful working relationships but despite that, few art and design courses truly replicate the procedure. Whilst there are relatively few courses in illustration compared to those teaching straight graphic design, there are even fewer that teach how to art direct. Most courses offer it, if at all, as part of their graphic design programme, without recognizing the breadth of the discipline. This is also true for advertising art direction, therefore many art directors have to learn on the job; some manage brilliantly, others not so well.

The approach to commissioning illustration for a newspaper or magazine art department is often dictated by the deadline, which is sometimes just a few days from the initial point of contact and/or briefing. There is scant time for meeting illustrators in the flesh when commissioning and the typical briefing is often far short of ideal.

Art directors or art editors normally call an illustrator directly, as many are unwilling to work with illustration agencies. Agents exist to represent the interests of the illustrator and will often attempt to increase a fee, however, in editorial work there is very little, if any, room for manoeuvre. Art directors rarely want this inconvenience, as there is little time for negotiation with a deadline approaching. Deadlines in editorial work are unforgiving; few other areas of the discipline work as rapidly.

'Due to massive increases in the number and circulation of digital and print newspapers and magazines, and the knock-on increase in feature or opinion-driven articles, there is a plethora of commissions available every month.'

3.2
Editorial illustration for
The Guardian newspaper.
Howard Read
Where photographs portray
fact in an editorial piece,
illustration can portray
personal viewpoints and ideas.

The brief

Much can happen between the initial brief and finished artwork. A good art director will, at the point of offering the work, have a brief or some copy to hand and be able to talk through the project. A brief may take different formats, but should include the following in addition to the text to be illustrated:
the size the image will run in publication,
the fee,
the deadline.

Less key, but still important, is knowing on which side of the page the illustration will fall. Whether it sits on the left or right page of the spread can influence how an image is constructed; a figure, for example, can be either positioned entering or exiting the publication.

In reality, the art director may have to wait for copy from the editor, cutting down the time the illustrator has to work on ideas and final artwork. A brief for an editorial commission is likely to be little more than an early version of the copy that can be subject to change and the illustrator may need to actively request the other details of the project. Requesting all information, including the fee and the deadline, must be undertaken before embarking on the project; if in doubt, ask the relevant questions.

Once underway, a commission usually involves two stages; creating a rough version, referred to as a sketch or visual, and then the final artwork. Illustrators have different approaches to how they start a job, but all agree that reading, digesting and understanding the brief is crucial. Before embarking on the illustration, the first step is to understand the publication. It is important to read previous copies to gauge the profile, look at who it is aimed at and research the title. Many illustrators will want to discuss with the art director why they have been chosen for the job, and ask if there was a particular piece of work or publicity that prompted the call. It is not unusual for a piece of previously printed publicity to be still working on their behalf five years later, are they still working in this particular way?

Some art directors can have very distinct ideas of how they expect the copy to be visualized, while others allow for an open interpretation by the illustrator. Keeping the art director informed will help ensure that there are no difficulties later in the project. Even if work cannot begin straight away, read the brief immediately upon receipt. This can help to throw up ideas, visual representations and overall elements that may appear in the illustration. Having the subject of the brief in the mind will be conducive to contemplating solutions, and will highlight any potential problems early in the process.

3.2

Research

Much of the enjoyment and challenge of working as an illustrator lies in understanding the subject of the text, as well as solving its visual interpretation.

Illustrators find that, within a relatively short period of time, they have to become an expert in the subject they are illustrating. The article may be about human relationships, neurosurgery, green politics, inner-city housing issues, car airbag systems or legal changes for solicitors; the possibilities are endless and flexibility in visualizing a range of subjects will be the key to working for a variety of publications.

Further research of subjects to gain a greater knowledge and understanding is part of the process. An article intended for publication may assume specialist knowledge from its intended audience – a specialist knowledge that the illustrator may have to rapidly get up to speed with.

Process

For illustrators working on editorial jobs, the first stage of creating visuals must come quickly. Ideas need to be visualized through sketching, mapping, doodling and drawing. Initial thoughts and ideas must be recorded as notes or lists as a useful starting point.

Art directors understand that not all illustrators work alike; they recognize that just because one likes to produce very finished and polished visuals there are others who scribble their intentions haphazardly, offering just a vague indication of how they intend to proceed. However roughs or visuals are produced, it is beneficial to all involved in the commission if much of the detail is resolved at this early stage. Failing to communicate the intentions of how the illustration will be executed, both conceptually and artistically, can lead to great problems further into the project.

3.3

A great idea only works if it communicates well and the visuals stage is the first real test of a concept and its validity. A good art director will view the visual through the eyes of the publication's readership to ensure that the image and concept will work. Building time into a project to allow for a rejection at the concept/visual stage is paramount; not all projects go according to the wishes of the illustrator.

It is important to create more than one idea at the initial stage; showing a favourite solution first can allow others to be held in reserve or the art director might want to see all options and make a choice from these. Creating just one concept always runs the risk of the project falling apart.

However it's arrived at, the point of executing the final artwork is another crucial aspect of any editorial job. Ensuring that the art director understands the method intended is important, particularly if the work uses a number of different media. If a commission has arisen from a photographic technique, for example, a similar technique must be employed in the final artwork as opposed to a more drawn or painterly approach – unless specifically requested. Not many art directors will be aware of every method that an illustrator employs, again this is a positive reason for clear lines of communication at the outset of the project. Positive surprises are the only surprises that an art director takes kindly to on the day of the deadline.

3.3
Illustration for John Lanchester's food column in *Esquire* magazine.
Mia Nilsson
Editorial work such as magazine and newspaper illustrations form the basis of many illustrators' workloads.

A typical editorial illustration timeline

Day	Magazine	Newspaper
1	Initial request from art director – checking availability of illustrator to undertake commission.	am: Initial request from art director. pm: Commission confirmed and full briefing given.
2	Commission confirmed and full briefing given via phone or email.	am: Research and initial ideas generation. pm: Further ideas generation and visualization.
3	Research and initial ideas generation.	am: Working up visuals. pm: Presentation of visuals to art director via email and follow-up phonecall.
4	Research and initial ideas generation.	Presentation of visuals to editor by art director and verbal feedback to illustrator.
5	Further ideas generation and visualization.	Presentation of second visuals and follow-up feedback.
6	Working up visuals.	Creation and presentation of final artwork.
7	Presentation of visuals to art director via email and follow-up phonecall.	
8	Presentation of visuals to editor by art director and verbal and/or written feedback to illustrator.	
9	Presentation of second visuals and follow-up feedback.	
10	Creation and presentation of final artwork.	

1. The illustrator as artist   2. The medium is the message   3. From outcomes to outlets   4. Communicating ideas   5. Making it happen   6. Production

← The overview   Editorial Illustration   Book publishing →

The editorial illustrator — an interview with Autumn Whitehurst

Editorial work for magazines and newspapers is the life-blood for many illustrators, allowing unique opportunities for showcasing new approaches and working methods. What is your take on this aspect of the industry and why is it important for you to participate in editorial illustration?

AW Editorial work is generally an illustrator's playground. Though it doesn't pay nearly as much as advertising work does, I find it to be the place in which I evolve. The clients are less inclined to define your approach so it's a great opportunity to really push yourself into fresh territory. This is very important to me because I have less and less free time in which to do work that allows me to explore my creative options.

You appear to have a very labour-intensive working method, could you describe the process, both conceptually and practically, of making your work?

AW The very first thing I do is lay out my sketches in Illustrator because it allows me to distort the elements until everything feels harmonious. The rendering work is done with Photoshop brushes, much like a painter would use paintbrushes, although painting digitally demands a different kind of precision due to the nature of the program. I then use photo references to help me understand how light wraps around the body, but beyond that it's up to my imagination, and much of my effort goes into making these figures long and sleek.

As far as concepts go, I respond to assignments with my intuition. If I have to think about it too hard, then I know that I've taken the wrong approach and that the illustration will be dead if I attempt to finish it. It's usually a particular kind of emotion that I'm after and the technique that I'm using lends itself to that. Highly narrative work is difficult to achieve because rendering the skin so heavily sets a kind of pace throughout the image that must be maintained. Even in an environment built up with line-work, everything needs to be very tight so it can be extremely time-consuming. This has been my motive for creating a second body of work that is simpler in its execution and this is what I'm slowly working towards.

Illustration can bring a different viewpoint from photography to a subject when used in a magazine. Your work sits quite firmly in the middle of these processes, at least in visual terms; how does that affect your interpretation of the brief/assignment?

AW I have to consider what I'm committing myself to in the initial stages because of the time involved in rendering the flesh, but there is also the pleasure of being able to take it a step further to create something that is almost like a fantasy, and this is liberating. I was concerned for a while about how close to photography some of the images were becoming, and wondered if it defeated the purpose of using illustration to accomplish what I was trying to achieve, but a friend pointed out that retouching a photo to such a degree would involve a lot more time than I was investing and that made me feel better about it.

By their very nature, magazines – and particularly newspapers – are only in the public eye for a short space of time and they have to relate to fashions and trends in image-making. How do you maintain an awareness of current design trends and keep one step ahead of the competition?

AW I can't deny how influential excellent work is in that it sets a standard I'd like to meet. I work the only way that I know how so I don't think much about trends. They seem a bit dangerous, because to follow them could end in career suicide once the industry decides to move on. It's very important to keep evolving my abilities and I find that this happens more so in the editorial work.

Please give a brief outline of your intentions when making illustrations for this sector of the industry?

AW I just want to make something as beautiful as I can within the given deadline so as to grab the readers' attention. Most of the commissions that I've been receiving are somehow fashion-related, so at the moment I'm concerned with creating images that have sex appeal. I want them to really sing, to be compositionally solid and ideally to suck the reader into a space that feels like a dream.

THE GUILTY BRIDE

HOW CAN A GIRL RAISED TO STAND ON HER OWN TWO FEET LEARN
TO STAND BY HER MAN? RACHAEL COMBE ON BECOMING A WIFE

s it so wrong to want a cake plate? What about matching cake pans, an electric hand mixer, and a double boiler? Is that, like, *wrong*? Once you have all that gear, is it so wrong to spend a whole afternoon baking a devil's food cake with marshmallow frosting that requires you to stand over the stove with the mixer on high speed, splattering boiling-hot corn syrup and egg whites all over your forearms? Is it wrong to then go out to three different stores to find the special little Cadbury chocolates that look like robins' eggs that they sell only at Easter and to arrange them in a flower pattern on top of your magnificent cake, which rests upon its sparkling pedestal? Is it wrong to then take pictures of the cake and spend a good five minutes just gazing at it, joyfully, reverently, imagining the delight of your dinner guests when they get a load of your magical, wondrous, unbelievable cake?

Because when I did this a few weeks ago and plopped it down on the table after dinner—voilà!—and my boyfriend, O., announced that I'd made it from scratch, our guests just looked at me blankly for a moment before someone said, "Uh, since when did you become Southern?" Then they all laughed. I blushed. It was not how I'd pictured the moment. I felt as though I'd been caught enacting a dirty fantasy.

And actually, I had been: You see, O. isn't my boyfriend anymore…he's my fiancé. We're getting married in August. The cake plate, the cake pans—all wedding gifts. And the role I was so eagerly trying on that night? Gracious hostess, princess bride, devoted wife. Nothing I've ever done has given me more of a thrill or caused me more shame.

I don't know which is worse: the baking or the wedding. Growing up under the tutelage of women who had only recently had their consciousness raised by Betty Friedan et. al., I was constantly reminded to avoid the sinkhole of domesticity. "Never learn to cook, girls," one of my friends' mothers used to warn us. "Because if you do, that's all you'll do for the rest of your life." Still, that doesn't fully explain my discomfort. With college, graduate school, and 10 years of a publishing career under my belt, I'm unlikely to find my options reduced to a skillet and a spatula anytime soon.

And while "Consumerism before feminism" could easily be the motto of the exploding domestic porn market and the wedding industry (or as O. calls it, the Marital Industrial Complex), that's a battle I've been fighting (and losing) with myself for years. Barneys would be a lot poorer and Planned Parenthood a lot richer if I always put my

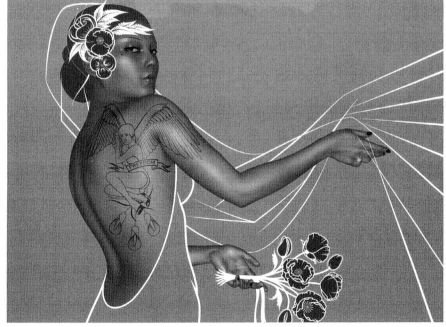

3.4
'The Guilty Bride', for monthly fashion Magazine *Elle UK*.
Autumn Whitehurst
Despite an intensive and time-consuming working method, Autumn Whitehurst strives to create editorial illustrations that capture a sense of place, that have an atmosphere, a sex appeal and are 'compositionally solid'.

1. The illustrator as artist   2. The medium is the message   3. From outcomes to outlets   4. Communicating ideas   5. Making it happen   6. Production

← The overview   Editorial illustration   Book publishing →

Book publishing

Arguably, the book was the first true medium for illustrators, and the relationship between written language and the illustrated image is a special one. This began with the illuminated religious manuscripts created between the seventh and ninth centuries, and continued with the birth of print in 1455. Until the invention of the camera and photography in 1839, illustration was the only form that printed images could take. Since photographic representation became the norm, the popularity of the illustrated image has been in decline. Within publishing now, the sectors most responsive to the work of illustrators are those of children's books, fiction titles and sometimes technical reference books, although increasingly these have turned towards using photography.

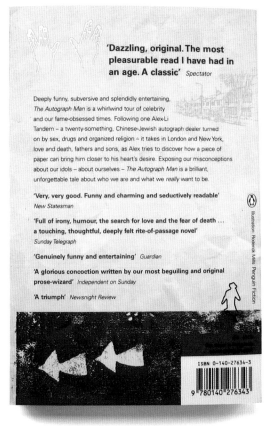

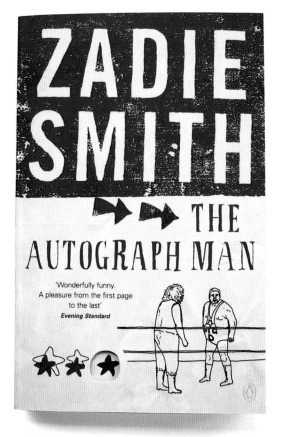

3.5

Children's books

There is, for many illustrators, something quite unique about creating illustrations for books. Now, illustrators are generally commissioned to either create entire children's books, often writing as well as illustrating the stories, or to produce front cover or jacket illustrations. Both areas can offer extremely rewarding commissions, artistically if not financially, as often there is a reasonable amount of time in which to produce the work. If working on a cover for a fiction title, there is often enough time to read the manuscript fully and produce first stage visuals before embarking upon the final artwork.

The visuals expected for illustrated book titles differ from newspaper and magazine commissions; artists are required to create very finished early versions of what will become the final artwork. The visuals will detail the position of every element within an image and will also include very detailed finished drawings of each of the book's central characters.

For the writer/illustrator working on both text and image for a children's title, there is a much longer lead-in time. The first stage of the process, following the initial briefing, leads to the creation of a number of dummy spreads that are presented at trade book fairs to gauge the appeal and the reaction to the concept, style and approach of the book. Feedback given now can be just the first of many stages in a long line that may influence the direction that the book begins to take.

3.5
Jacket design for adult fiction
The Autograph Man by Zadie
Smith (Penguin, 2003).
Roderick Mills
Illustrators are frequently
commissioned for both book
covers and internal illustrations
to accompany text.

Artistic and editorial control

A book requires far more financial investment from a publishing company than any output from an editorial publisher, particularly now, with the rise of digital publishing. In order to recoup the initial expenses and move into creating a profit, books are expected to sell for a far longer period of time than the day or the month that a newspaper or magazine is on the shelf for. Ensuring that the product suits the intended audience, continues to sell after the publication date and remains relevant and fresh are all aspects that publishers take very seriously. With greater financial and commercial risk, it is understandable that greater artistic and editorial control rests with the publisher.

Art direction during the development of a book can come from many quarters. The art director or designer will view every illustration during a project and so too will the book's editor and editorial team, as essentially the initial commission can have come from either department. Equally important within the process, are the thoughts and comments of the marketing department, since marketing plays a huge role in determining the success of a book. Books can sell or be left on the shelf depending on public reaction to the cover, and increasingly little is left to chance in this area. Feedback will reflect the saleability of the book's design. Requests from marketing and sales departments may include changes to colours, increases in type sizes and the inclusion of particular images.

One further aspect of what may seem an elongated process of commission can come into play even after every other department has approved both the illustration and the design of a book. Well-known authors can demand approval rights for any jacket designs for their works and, despite being a rare occurrence, can send any jacket back to the drawing board.

Understanding the context of the book both artistically and commercially, the visual translation of the text as well as the overall creation of a design that appeals to an audience, are both fundamental aspects of successful book illustration.

1. The illustrator as artist   2. The medium is the message   3. From outcomes to outlets   4. Communicating ideas   5. Making it happen   6. Production

← Editorial illustration   Book publishing   Fashion illustration →

The book illustrator — an interview with Sara Fanelli

Illustrations created for books play a huge role in bringing a text to life. How do you start the process of creating your images and, when you also create the text, which comes first?

SF   After reading the text, I ask myself what aspect or issue I wish to explore with the visual comment and try to portray that. When I work on children's stories often the idea starts from a visual image. As Quentin Blake said before, this is one great thing about being the author as well as the illustrator: you can write a story about things you like drawing.

Which illustrated children's books were important to you as a child and why?

SF   I loved the atmosphere of a book. I was mainly attracted to the world that was depicted and contained within, and how I could enter it. I feel very privileged now to have the chance to create such worlds for the imagination. I also enjoyed the colours and was fascinated by details, for example in looking for the reoccurring detail of the worm (in Italian 'Zigozago') in Richard Scarry's books. I also had a book with photographic illustrations and its unusual look was intriguing and special.

The illustrated book in its simplest form is a sequential set of images that correspond to a narrative – how do you decide which parts of the story need illustrating?

SF   I am not very interested in depicting exactly the same things that are described in the text. If the text is good it's better to let the words describe and suggest the image directly to the reader's imagination, and to offer instead a picture that shows a less obvious detail, or that gives an unexpected visual slant to the text.

The development of ideas and visuals is part of the working process for an illustrator; how many stages does your own work take and at what point do you show the publishers the work?

SF   It is important for me to have a clear idea of the book before speaking to a publisher. I am open to and welcome sensitive editorial input and I am aware that things will change after my initial presentation, but it is good to start with some certainties.

Some books take longer at the initial stage, but then progress smoothly and others, which at first seem smooth, might eventually take longer. It is a very organic process and it is important to have the ability to be open to the comments from editors whilst remaining clear about what the original vision and inspiration for the book was.

Can you give a brief outline of your intentions when making illustrations for this sector of the industry?

SF   I try to make a book as I like it and would have liked it as a child. I think books come out better this way than if one tries to guess what children would generally like in their books. There is enough of a child in ourselves to know what we liked when we were younger (and still like!), and enough of an adult in a child for them to know when someone is patronizing them.

1. The illustrator as artist   2. The medium is the message   **3. From outcomes to outlets**   4. Communicating ideas   5. Making it happen   6. Production

← Editorial illustration   Book publishing   Fashion illustration →

3.6
Jacket and page design for
children's fiction *Pinocchio*.
Sara Fanelli
A genuine twist on a children's
classic gave Sara Fanelli plenty
of scope to create a brand new
aesthetic for this popular story.
For the cover, Sara created
a slipcase that produces an
animation as the book is pulled
out. As the book comes out,
Pinocchio's nose grows!

3.7
'I can't stop thinking about myself'. One of four illustrations created for *Monki Magazine*.
Annelie Carlström
For illustrators not trained in fashion design it is wise to undertake serious research before embarking on fashion commissions.

Fashion illustration

For some, the term illustration is synonymous with the work of fashion illustrators, despite it losing much ground to photography since its height of popularity in the 1930s. Fashion illustration has moved gradually away from documenting the work of fashion designers for magazines, although sketched images have remained the starting point for many fashion designers as they visualize on paper the structure and fabrics for the garments that they are designing.

For the illustrator not trained as a fashion designer who wants to work in this field, it is wise to undertake the discipline with a clear understanding of who to approach for commissions, as opportunities may be less visibly flagged than in other areas of the discipline.

Opportunities

Occasionally art directors cut against the tide of photographic imagery to offer illustrators the opportunity to create fresher, more personal interpretations of the season's trends and ranges. This type of fashion story commission usually comes from the fashion monthlies. It's mainly the more upmarket magazines as well as men's titles that tend to opt for this approach. The more avant-garde and independent the title, the more they are expected to be directional in their approach; in fact it is this type of fashion illustration that is considered to lead the entire discipline stylistically.

Outside of the fashion and 'style' press, the recent rise in the recognition of fashion illustration can be attributed to a number of independent clothing labels, as well as bigger brands with an understanding of marketing to youth audiences.

Cult clothing labels such as A Bathing Ape in Japan, Silas in the UK and Huntergatherer in the US all began to use illustration in original and fresh ways that led some larger corporate companies to follow suit. Nike, Adidas, Levi's and Diesel have all developed ranges of clothing with print graphics inspired or created by contemporary illustrators, or they've led marketing and advertising campaigns using the work of contemporary illustrators.

In a route similar to that of successful fashion photographers, many illustrators have started by creating low-fee, directional images for magazines, viewing them as a testing ground for their work. The transition to creating advertising and publicity for fashion labels with greater budgets and fees proves that their work has appeal and longevity. Longevity in fashion, however, may not last much longer than a couple of seasons.

1. The illustrator as artist 2. The medium is the message 3. From outcomes to outlets 4. Communicating ideas 5. Making it happen 6. Production

← Book publishing | Fashion illustration | Advertising illustration →

'Nike, Adidas, Levi's and Diesel have all developed ranges of clothing with print graphics inspired or created by contemporary illustrators…'

Illustration and textile designs

Freelance textile designers endure a particularly subservient role in the fashion industry. Their designs are often sold for very small fees with no retention of copyright. For the illustrator that moves into producing textile designs, the payment and ownership terms can come as a genuine surprise. It is, perhaps, the enjoyment of working for another type of client in another medium that inspires most to work in this area, rather than any commercial gain. For those illustrators whose work is successful and has a high recognition factor, an invitation to create textile designs may help to ensure better rates and even the retention of copyright ownership.

Successful illustrators working across a range of textile applications have recently witnessed great interest in their work, some being commissioned to produce entire collections for fashion companies and labels. As illustration in this sector gathers greater recognition, so the scope of projects increases. With public interest in property, architecture and interiors escalating in recent years, it has come as no surprise that some fashion companies have turned their attention to a bigger canvas than the body. Many have seamlessly launched their own home interiors ranges and illustrators have capitalized by creating textile designs for duvet covers, curtains, wallpapers and towels. As fashion design has moved across the divide from clothing and into the home, so too has the flexibility and creativity of today's fashion illustrators.

3.8
Yellow Field print, for Cacharel.
Petra Börner
With new, fast digital processes, illustrations can be efficiently applied to textiles. Here, Petra Börner's Yellow Field print has been used for Cacharel's 'Cocoa Bean' dress in their A/W06 collection.

3.8

The fashion illustrator — an interview with Stina Persson

Illustration and fashion are inextricably linked and in recent years the relationship between the two has blossomed further. Why do you think this has happened and how does your work fit into this relationship?

SP   I think the balance between the use of photography and illustration in the fashion world was off for quite some time. Art directors and editors at magazines seemed to be scared of illustration and the element of unexpectedness that it brings. But now that everything is digital and can be controlled and manipulated, maybe the longing for the uncontrolled has come back.

The figure plays a prominent role in much of your work, how crucial is drawing from life, even outside of your commissioned work?

SP   Drawing from life is necessary to train your eye. And that's what it's all about; a good eye. On the other hand it's both a luxury and time consuming. Therefore I, as I think most illustrators do today, work from flat reference material, such as magazine clippings, photographs or even digital snapshots of posing family and friends. After all, there are deadlines to meet.

Fashion can be a notoriously fickle industry and with your work appearing in numerous major publications and for numerous companies, how do you ensure that it remains fresh and forward-looking?

SP   To keep work fresh is one of my biggest struggles as I think that this either makes or breaks the final piece. And it's not always easy in a commercial world when ten people have different ideas of how a hand should be held or what percentage of magenta a watercolour shade should be in. But that's also the challenge of creating work commercially.

My way to deal with this has been to do several drawings until one feels fresh and quick. It should look effortless. Which takes… effort. If it doesn't happen on one piece of paper I assemble the final piece digitally from several drawings.

More generally, consciously keeping my style modern and up-to-date is not my main aim – there are so many other illustrators who are amazing at it. I just try to do what I'm doing and not get stuck in a routine. If it looks modern to people, that's good.

Do you approach illustration projects with any predetermined notions of how the finished piece will work and how many attempts do you create before you are happy with the results?

SP   I wish I didn't have to have a finished image in my head as I work – so that you could always be open to what the piece needs and ready to make something cool out of a mistake. But commercially that wouldn't work as you have to submit first a rough sketch and later a finished sketch. I've almost succeeded in convincing my clients that the rough really is just rough for me, as the finished image is done in watercolour and needs to be at least a little unpredictable.

Can you give a brief outline of your intentions when making illustrations for this sector of the industry?

SP   I've somehow found myself in a special niche of fashion illustration that I think sometimes is forgotten. Since fashion illustration became 'in vogue' again a lot of companies and publications not dealing in fashion directly have started to want some of that fashion look to rub off on them. This is what I've done to a large extent; a lot of fashionable-looking work, only a small part of which is directly related to the fashion industry. Instead, I've worked for everyone from Volvo to French aperitifs… Maybe this extended use of fashion illustration also adds to the feeling that fashion illustration is everywhere.

1. The illustrator as artist   2. The medium is the message   3. From outcomes to outlets   4. Communicating ideas   5. Making it happen   6. Production

← Book publishing   Fashion illustration   Advertising illustration →

Advertising illustration

Advertising is a tough sector to break into and is not for the faint-hearted; it can be a brutal environment for the freelance illustrator. In return for punishing schedules, unrealistic deadlines, lack of creative decision-making and being told what to do and sometimes how to do it, there is, however, the promise of the advertising fee. It is generally recognized that an increase in fees equates to the increased pressure felt when undertaking most advertising commissions.

Agency structures

All advertising agencies are structurally similar. Within the art department an art director will work hand-in-hand with a copywriter under the head of art or the creative director, normally responsible for a number of similar two-person creative teams/partnerships. Art directors create the visual properties whilst the copywriter creates the written word or spoken script, for any advertising campaign.

Working alongside the art department of an advertising agency is the art-buying department. This manages the freelance sources of artwork: the photographers, model-makers, directors, animators and illustrators. The art buyer keeps abreast of developments, trends, fashions and movements in each of the key disciplines by attending exhibition openings, scouring the art and design press and constantly calling in portfolios of work from individual practitioners and agencies representing the best in contemporary work.

The account handler ensures the relationship between the advertising agency and the client runs smoothly; their main role is to liaise and coordinate each project for the agency and client. They are also responsible for making presentations of creative work to the client, sometimes without a member of the creative team and certainly always without the illustrator present. Sitting outside of the creative loop can lead to frustration for the freelance illustrator; client responses, changes and alterations to visuals or artwork are all relayed via the account handler. Be warned, this is a line of communication longer than the illustrator may find beneficial.

3.9
'Think About it' by Kia Motors. Press, web and TV advertising.
Pete Fowler for Mustoes Design Agency
Pete Fowler was commissioned to create a range of applications that were used in various media across the campaign.

Coverage

A strong advertising campaign will aim to immerse itself and the product into the public's subconscious. It will seek to present an idea and an image for that product that becomes instantly recognizable, creating brand awareness and a product personality. Advertising utilizes a range of media in its pursuit of brand/product recognition: from posters on billboards, bus sides and shelters, referred to as 'outdoor media', to TV and cinema commercials known as 'on-air media'. The scope is endless and to the illustrator working on an advertising campaign, the effect of such coverage can be enormous.

In recent years, campaigns have become less regional and more international. With increased outlets for advertising, there is greater public recognition of campaigns and the associated product. Running hand-in-hand with this are the associations made with the illustration style and the visual identity of the campaign. This can be hugely beneficial if the product is deemed 'cool' or has entered the public zeitgeist as it encourages other companies to commission the same illustrator, hoping for associations to be made.

More frequent though, is the downside; the work remains connected to a product long after any advertising campaign has ceased to run. This stylistic link can prove detrimental to bringing in new advertising commissions; the visual associations with previous products being too strong to risk attempting to create new ones. This can mean that even the hardest working illustrators are only likely to be commissioned for very visible campaigns every other year at the most.

Steep learning curves

Advertising offers many unique challenges; most too must be resolved within an incredibly short time-span. An advertising art director may view a portfolio of illustration work but see the potential, for example, in using the artist for a TV commercial. This may be despite the illustrator having little or no direct previous involvement in animation.

She or he may be called upon to work on ideas, themes and storyboards for an animated commercial and if the initial stage is successful, the illustrator may then be required to embark on a collaboration throughout the project with an animation house. Most illustrators enjoy rising to this type of challenge in the pursuit of creative work.

1. The illustrator as artist 2. The medium is the message **3. From outcomes to outlets** 4. Communicating ideas 5. Making it happen 6. Production

← Fashion illustration Advertising illustration Music industry illustration →

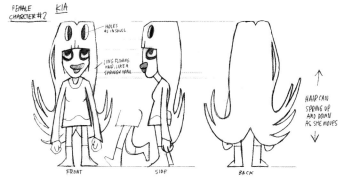

FEMALE CHARACTER #2   KIA

HOLES AS IN SKULL

LONG FLOWING HAIR LIKE A SPRINGY TRAIL

HAIR CAN SPRING UP AND DOWN AS SHE MOVES

FRONT   SIDE   BACK

3.9

3.10
'Think About it' by Kia Motors.
Press, web and TV advertising.
Pete Fowler for Mustoes Design Agency
A project of this complexity needs time and extremely well-coordinated organization.

Advertising fees

Once a portfolio of work has been reviewed and its creator seen as potentially the right candidate for the project, a period of negotiation will commence. Very rarely does the agency reveal the fee that they wish to pay for the work at the outset. A normal discussion about the payment for the job will start with the agency detailing the client, the product, the number of images required, the media that the work is expected to run across, the period of time that the work will be used for and the deadline for delivery. Any one or combination of these factors can affect the outcome of the discussions.

Quoting for work

Creating a quotation for a job will often require meticulous planning with attention to the smallest detail. It can be a time-consuming task – one good reason why many illustrators work through an agent – and the lengthy task of creating a quote will not always result in the job being commissioned.

Test images and pitching

Increasingly, not only does the illustrator have to win the job on merit – he or she can now be asked to provide a test image. A test should not be confused with a first stage visual; it is an opportunity for the agency to request an image, with no usage attached, to gauge how the illustrator might tackle the job if given it. The fee for a test image is invariably low despite sometimes taking as long to create as a final illustration.

Similar to the test image is the pitch, which can be either paid or unpaid. Most pitching for work is undertaken by advertising agencies and design companies, but the knock-on effect ensures that illustrators are being commissioned to create images for these pitches. Low fees without any guarantee of a real project, equate to a risk being carried by the illustrator as well as the design or advertising group.

Focus groups

Even after submission of the test image, it can still take an agency and client some time to come to a final decision. Many clients, unwilling to trust their instincts, decide to test the work using a focus group, where the general public is used for market research. Illustration fares particularly badly in these tests, as the general public is generally unaware of how the discipline works or how to rationalize its response to it.

1. The illustrator as artist 2. The medium is the message **3. From outcomes to outlets** 4. Communicating ideas 5. Making it happen 6. Production

← Fashion illustration Advertising illustration Music industry illustration →

3.10

The advertising illustrator — an interview with Henry Obasi

Working as an illustrator on advertising commissions puts your work in front of a massive audience; do you find this a creative challenge or is it like any other project?

HO   This can be regarded as a challenge but not a major one. No matter how large the audience, advertising companies usually commission specific illustrators to engage with a target-specific audience. This is mainly because they are aware of the audience's social and cultural characteristics and how that audience will respond to the artist's visual style. Most of the pressure to define the audience has been taken off by this stage of commissioning.

Advertising is seen as the most financially rewarding sector for an illustrator to work in; what are the other benefits you can relate to?

HO   Advertising campaigns provide a clearly-defined audience to view your work on a larger platform (usually internationally, or at the very least, nationally). Having your work seen by both a global and national audience in one hit is one of the most gratifying accolades. Working with a large brand gives the chance of my illustration being seen worldwide, and this elevates my status as an illustrator as you become recognizable beyond the small arenas of popular culture. This also brings me to the attention of possible overseas clients. It is very hard to divorce the financial rewards of doing a large advertising campaign from anything else because all the benefits feed each other.

3.11
'Goal'. Press advertising for Orange.
Henry Obasi for Mother
Here, using an illustrator has allowed Orange to reference major sports figures without problems of sponsorship or image rights.

You've produced work for a range of advertising clients – does it mean that your work becomes synonymous with the brands that you've helped to advertise?

HO   If you have worked primarily with one brand in particular, it is common sense that the audience will naturally associate the illustrator with that brand. But more importantly, other brands will associate you with that brand. This can be both a blessing and a curse, especially with fashion brands, where competition is fierce.

I did a high profile campaign for a fashion label a few years ago. The exposure was good and the campaign lasted a while, but this had the detrimental effect of aligning my illustration style with that label. It became increasingly obvious that it would be a while before I would be able to work with another big fashion brand, especially as my style of illustration is considered niche. However, the plus side was that other big brands from different market sectors noticed my work and subsequently commissioned me. Working on a major ad campaign had given me validation, in their eyes.

Advertising deadlines are often very short. Do you adjust your working methods to suit this and how many stages does your work go through for advertising clients?

HO   Workflow now has had to change from the old days. It is no longer possible to spend three months painting the figurehead of a bank for a corporate brochure. The working process for creating images is of paramount importance in an arena where reception to visual stimuli is instantaneous and then forgotten. This digital age has forced the viewer, be it the art director, client or target audience, to expect visual data almost immediately.

Most illustrators have now adapted their style to fit a more speedy workflow. Initially I created all my illustrations using a mixture of drawing and screenprinting, but I soon found that this was not time-effective (or, more seriously, cost-effective). When you have clients requesting amendments every five minutes you have to up your game! At that time there were almost five different stages to my working process and each stage was nearly a day long. Now I have got it down to two or three stages that last a fraction of the time. I can complete a commission from rough to finish in anything from a couple of hours to a couple of days.

Can you give a brief outline of your intentions when making illustrations for this sector of the industry?

HO I need to try and communicate some of my own messages through my work, whether stylistically through mark-making or through art directive interplay. By this I mean being involved in the communicative process of a campaign. Usually art directors commission illustrators to re-dress their rather fixed ideas. This position of no-involvement relegates the illustrator to no more than decorator. At times this is cool – sometimes the advertising message being communicated is ultra specific. The fear of any external factors being brought into the mix by the illustrator can be perceived as possibly being detrimental, especially when big bucks are involved. But when the illustrator is given a chance to inject artistic quality other than their drawing style, it is a bonus.

When working with Mother on a campaign for Orange, I was able to express humour in my work. By being involved from the initial stages I could introduce creative elements. As with most artists, all illustrators want to be recognized at some level and that is no different for me. I want people to see my work and enjoy it at the very least. If the campaign works and gets people to spend their money, then that is a bonus!

3.11

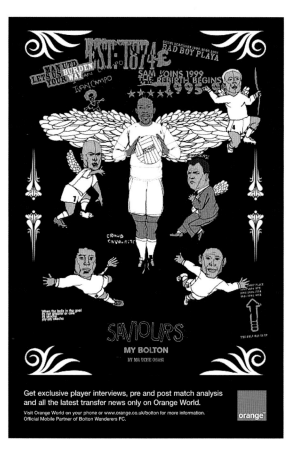

Music industry illustration

For many, illustration is seen as the discipline that visualizes text, but another key aspect lies in its ability to give music a visual form.

Music graphics have played a definitive role in shaping the way that we relate to the music that we hear, creating an identity and personality for the product in a visual form. Long gone are the days when record companies could simply create an album sleeve by using a photograph of the artist alone on the cover. Far more unique and sophisticated solutions aid sales through sleeve design that projects a graphic image of the artist.

Record label set-ups

The music business is a global industry that employs tens of thousands of people and represents artists and acts that generate many millions of dollars per annum. The huge scale of the operation means that finding in-roads into working as a freelance illustrator can be less than straightforward. Large record labels normally run their own art departments, creating sleeves and promos for their acts in-house, buying in photography and illustration on a project-by-project basis. Some of the large labels, however, prefer to out-source all of their design, working with one major design company or a selection of smaller agencies, commissioning them for the entire design and production of each project.

3.12

Gaining access to information and contact details for both record label art departments and independent design companies, although not initially as simple as in other sectors of the design and advertising industries, will prove fruitful. A little more 'homework', coupled with an awareness of current and emerging trends in both music and design practice within the discipline is necessary. Frequent visits to record stores and regular checking of the small-print credits in the sleeve notes will elicit the correct contact information, or at least work as a starting point. Increasingly, individual acts now have their own website where further contact information can be obtained.

It is rare for an illustrator to work for a particular band throughout their entire lifespan, but it can happen. Creating images for merchandise, back-drops and set design, as well as animations for the band's promo videos are all areas that can open up for those whose work defines the graphic look of a recording artist.

3.12
'Mish mash' club poster for Cargo nightclub.
Insect
Many independent record labels and clubs require promotional material and this can be an interesting, if not lucrative, field to gain valuable experience in.

1. The illustrator as artist   2. The medium is the message   3. From outcomes to outlets   4. Communicating ideas   5. Making it happen   6. Production

← Advertising illustration   Music industry illustration   Studio collaboration →

Working for the music industry brings another dimension to the job of the illustrator who is normally associated with bringing text to life. In this sector it is about bringing a visual form to music and it can also be associated with fashions and trends. How do you respond to a given project?

KS   Well, it really depends on the project. Sometimes the client is open and sometimes they come with a clearly thought-out idea. Both are fine with me. Of course I prefer illustrating the music I like, but sometimes it can be really refreshing to do something completely different.

Record sleeve design has been a vital aspect of marketing music; when CDs emerged to replace vinyl, the canvas reduced dramatically. Do you enjoy the restrictions of the medium?

KS   I still prefer vinyl format and fortunately I've been working with record companies who usually publish in vinyl too. Now, the clumsy CD jewel case may be a classic, but I usually prefer the cardboard ones. It really is a challenge to make the small CD format appealing. But I wonder what we are going to do with MP3s?

3.13

The audience's perception of a musician or recording artist is often drawn from the graphics created for their recordings – do you have the artist's visual identity in mind whilst you create their cover art?

KS   Sure. But I prefer covers that take the listener to a different level. I think the covers can be a bit challenging too – I always try to illustrate the moods and feelings from the music. Of course, it's just my personal view, but I hope it opens the music up to other people too.

Your work has a surreal, other-worldly feel about it – do you think that it has helped you get work in this area of design?

KS   Well, it's really difficult to say. Sometimes the music makes me draw different things. It's really about the music and how it matches with the illustration. Hopefully one day I can do a project where the image is first.

Can you give a brief outline of your intentions when making illustrations for this sector of the industry?

KS   Well, first, hopefully I like the music I'm going to illustrate. If I do, I usually get stuck into it for some time. And then I get deeper and try to understand it. After that it's easy and inspiring to make my work. But if I don't like the stuff – then it's like any other work project, good or bad, but I don't take it too personally.

1. The illustrator as artist   2. The medium is the message   3. From outcomes to outlets   4. Communicating ideas   5. Making it happen   6. Production

← Advertising illustration   Music industry illustration   Studio collaboration →

3.13
Country Falls CD cover design.
Husky Rescue, Catskills Records.
Kustaa Saksi
Surreal landscapes and imagery
represent the *Country Falls* album
artwork for Husky Rescue.

Studio collaboration

Whilst many aspects of the communication design industry are contained within specialized compartments and departments, as we have seen with advertising, magazine, newspaper and book publishing, there are a vast number of design companies that exist to offer broader services.

Independent graphic design studios and companies far outnumber the specialist advertising agencies or publishing companies, and are a rich source of work for the illustrator. Commissions can be forthcoming for any type of project; illustrators are called in to create images for annual reports, to work on logo designs, produce cover illustrations for financial reports, artwork for theatre posters – the list is endless. As in other aspects of the industry, knowing the specialist nature of each company is vital before approaching them with requests for meetings or portfolio reviews. Following the international design press and researching company websites is the best way of gleaning up-to-date information about projects undertaken by these independent companies.

Working relationships

The working relationship for both illustrator and the design company is an important one and much of the success in any collaboration relies on a level of trust between both parties. For the designer commissioning the illustrator, he or she must feel confident that the work is delivered within the deadline and is of a standard that matches previous work in the artist's portfolio. The illustrator must trust that the designer will use his or her work in a respectful and professional way; not running type over an image or cropping off the sides of the artwork without prior consultation.

Working relationships can take time to build, but the key to ensuring a project runs smoothly lies in open lines of communication; regular conversations on the phone or via email to update the designer on how the illustration is taking shape can be very useful.

It is wise, when working for a new client, to build into the schedule an extra stage to show the artwork in progress. This stage sits between the viewing of the visuals and the artwork, and can be used to ensure that all elements within the image are present and correct. Some illustrators produce a black-and-white line version of their intended artwork to help the designer visualize how the final illustration will look.

3.14
Alpha and Bravo – Skyflyers,
British Airways.
Tado for Fitch International
These two characters were used extensively throughout the Skyflyers branding, merchandise and marketing, both in print and online. Life-size mascots of the characters were also created for promotional events.

Contracts and purchase orders

To ensure that both parties fully understand the process of the commission, it can be useful for a contract or purchase order to be issued by the design company to the illustrator. Incorporated into the contract must be a description of the job itself, the fee, the deadline for submission of the work, as well as payment terms and conditions.

Unfortunately, not every company adheres to the principle of the contract or purchase order, and practice across the industry varies. It is rare, for example, for a magazine in the UK to issue a purchase order, but standard practice for a similar company in the US. The purchase order, or PO, exists to protect both the client and illustrator. A signed PO ensures that the artist can invoice for the fee agreed at the start of the job and that is documented on the paperwork. This method avoids the need to rely on word-of-mouth or vague recollection of the details of any discussion, and is useful for commissions that may run into weeks or even months. Good practice means that an accounts department will not have to seek authorization to make a payment after the invoice has arrived if a contract or PO number is quoted on the invoice.

The contract and the PO are really ways of standardizing written agreements. If the company does not have templates for these available, ask for the agreement in writing, as a formality.

'Independent graphic design studios and companies far outnumber the specialist advertising agencies or publishing companies, and are a rich source of work for the illustrator.'

1. The illustrator as artist 2. The medium is the message 3. From outcomes to outlets 4. Communicating ideas 5. Making it happen 6. Production

← Music industry illustration Studio collaboration Self-initiated illustration →

The collaborative illustrator — an interview with Anthony Burrill

Working with design companies differs from working in other sectors of the market – there is more crossover and collaboration between designer and illustrator/image-maker. How do you feel that this has benefitted your work?

AB When working for an ad agency the traditional hierarchies are well understood by everybody involved. Normally I have the most contact with the art director during the job. The agency then deals with the client; there isn't much direct communication. When working with design companies there tends to be much more contact with everybody involved. It feels like there is much more collaboration. Projects tend to develop at a slower pace with design companies. There are more stages involved and a greater lead-in time to production. I feel that clients get more out of me when I'm more involved in the project, rather than just being a stylist.

At what stage in a project do you ideally like to be involved and how many stages do you normally envisage a project taking?

AB Ideally, I'd like to be involved right at the start. In practice it tends to be quite a long way in. Sometimes you are asked to pitch for a job. I don't think anybody enjoys pitching for work; I try to avoid it if possible. Sometimes people pay for pitches, which helps the motivation and it feels more 'real'. That helps you to get thinking about a project. Usually the pitch work doesn't take that long. If there is a small shortlist of possible designers, it shouldn't be too hard to pick the right person for the job. After the pitch has been won it starts getting busy. Initial designs from the pitch have to be resolved and ideas have to be developed. If there are questions about style, these have to be addressed too. After this initial stage there are usually another couple of rounds of revisions before final designs are presented. There are inevitable tweaks to be made on the final designs. This is usually the point where very tight deadlines get stretched a bit!

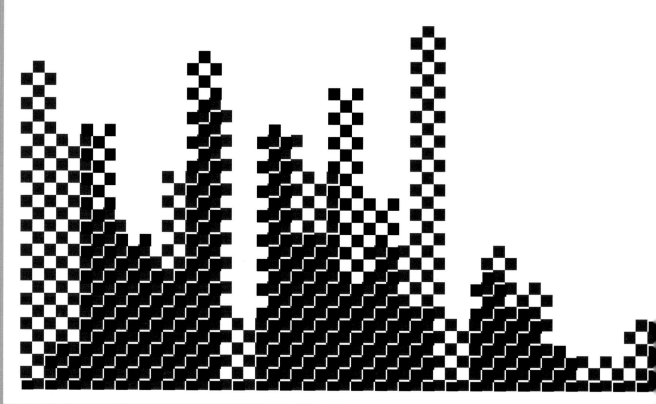

Pricing work for projects with design companies is not nearly as simple as in editorial or even advertising work – how do you find a happy medium?

AB Most projects tend to be priced as a single design fee, rather than a daily rate. People in design always ask me what my daily rate is. I don't have one. The fee depends on the size of the project, the usage and the client. Advertising tends to be more generous, but then the pressures and deadlines are always much greater with advertising.

What freedom does working with design companies on projects allow and how does your own interpretation of the brief lead the working process that you adopt?

AB I am normally approached to work on a project as a result of people seeing my previous work – so usually there is an understanding that they want my particular approach. I try to think of new ways of doing things for each project. Sometimes this doesn't work, then people ask me to do something that I've already done before. Every job involves compromise on both parts. The client has a strong idea of what they want and understands the audience they are talking to. At the end of the project I'm always happy if I've managed to produce a piece of work that feels like it's been the result of a good collaboration between me and the client.

Can you give a brief outline of your intentions when making work for this sector of the industry?

AB I don't really tend to approach work for design companies in a different way to any other client. The main thing for me is to have a good dialogue with the client.

3.15
Mural for Bloomberg. Design studio collaboration.
Anthony Burrill for Scarlet Projects
Burrill was commissioned to create a mural for Bloomberg, at the financial institution's headquarters in London. Vinyl graphics were applied directly to the walls, although the design was resolved on-screen prior to installation.

Self-initiated illustration

Every illustrator enjoys the prospect of working outside of what constitutes a 'standard' commission. For some it can be frustrating to find that after a couple of years of regular work, commissions start to become repetitive or even mundane. Keeping things alive and fresh can take the illustrator into new areas of interest and can help push one or two boundaries at the edges of the discipline.

A progressive approach to illustration can be achieved by continuing to work independently in sketchbooks, creating new artwork and generally spending time researching and exploring new ways of visualizing and new forms of expression.

Finding time to work on self-initiated projects can be problematic when an illustrator is busy with art directors and designers requesting commissions, but it is crucial in keeping one step ahead of the game. It may be as simple as taking a morning out of the studio each week to visit exhibitions and galleries, or an afternoon drawing on location. It may be a local life-drawing class or a print workshop, either way it can help feed the imagination, give some perspective to the activity of illustration and assist in finding new directions to work in and towards.

Self-initiated work can often lead to commercial spin-off projects. An illustrator's desire to work in new and different areas of interest or pure financial necessity are both strong drivers for self-initiated work. Organizing an independent exhibition of new work is a useful way of keeping clients informed about developments in a body of work and can be financially positive if sales are accomplished. Creating limited-edition screen-prints or digital prints can mean that prices per unit can be kept reasonably low, but profits can accumulate when an image is sold numerous times.

Illustrators with an eye for both fashion and business find that investing time and capital into designing and producing a small range of T-shirts can be another form of income. Small, independent fashion retail outlets will often take a range of T-shirts on a sale-or-return basis and this experience can be helpful when approaching fashion companies and labels for freelance commissions.

A growth area in recent years has been in the production of 'toys'. Originally starting as promotional devices for independent record and fashion labels, a sizable interest has grown in limited-edition toy characters. Created for and aimed at an adult audience who have grown up with toy figures based on characters from movies, animations, comics and video games, the new genre concentrates on hipper, more streetwise and stylistically cool figures. Often starting life as 2D sketches within illustrators' sketchbooks or in commissioned artwork, these toys have gone from purely promotional items to desirable, collectable objects.

'Keeping things alive and fresh can take the illustrator into new areas of interest and can help push one or two boundaries at the edges of the discipline.'

3.16
'Forest'. Self-initiated illustration.
Mark Boardman
It is often hard to find time for self-initiated work, but it can be incredibly rewarding and will often open new doors and break new boundaries.

3.16

1. The illustrator as artist   2. The medium is the message   3. From outcomes to outlets   4. Communicating ideas   5. Making it happen   6. Production

← Studio collaboration   Self-initiated illustration   Case study: Olivier Kugler →

The self-initiating illustrator – an interview with Han Hoogerbrugge

Personal work can be the driving influence for commercial projects; how do you maintain the correct balance?

HH   My personal work and commercial work are often close together. I get asked for commissions because of what I do with my free work and I can only do commercial jobs if they relate to my free work. Usually clients are after something kind of dark, funny and different when they commission me. This means I don't have to worry about a balance most of the time. The commercial work usually feels like the same thing as my free work.

Does your working method alter depending on the type of project – personal or commercial – that you are working on?

HH   No, I do what I do and I think that's one of the main reasons people ask me. It is definitely one of my demands when taking on a commercial job. I need to have the freedom to do things my way. Of course I listen to a client's needs and I try to give them what they want, but it should all stay within the range of the kind of thing I do.

What themes and ideas do you explore in your own work that translate to commercial projects?

HH   I try to communicate uncertain feelings with my work. Although my work is usually black and white, the ideas behind the work are grey. If I make an animation with a smoking character, it shouldn't be clear if I'm against smoking or pro smoking. There should be a little of both in it. I try to leave room for the viewer to find their own personal interpretation. In the end, its meaning is decided by the viewer. Commercial work usually needs clear communication, but I always try to insert some of my greyness in it. At first the message might be clear, but on a closer look you might see something less clear.

Can you give a brief outline of your intentions when making illustrations for this sector of the industry?

HH   Making money is my prime intention; if I could make enough money with my own work I probably wouldn't do commercial stuff. On the other hand, it's nice to do something else every once in a while. Working on your own stuff all the time can make you blind. Commercial jobs can create a healthy distance between me and my work, and give me a better perspective on what I do – but then again, if it didn't make me money, I wouldn't do it.

3.17
HAFF Leader, Holland Animation Film Festival. Film festival promo.
Han Hoogerbrugge
Han Hoogerbrugge, based in Holland, creates self-initiated, and challenging and often controversial animations that he releases online through his own website. Putting himself at the centre of his work, Hoogerbrugge uses digital photographic self-portraits as a trace-guide for his Flash-animated drawings.

1. The illustrator as artist   2. The medium is the message   3. From outcomes to outlets   4. Communicating ideas   5. Making it happen   6. Production

← Studio collaboration   Self-initiated illustration   Case study: Olivier Kugler →

3.17

Case study: Olivier Kugler

Olivier Kugler was born in 1970 in Stuttgart, Germany. Influenced by the French/Belgian Bande Desinées and Otto Dix, he now works as an illustrator for clients all over the world, including *XXI*, Süddeutsche Zeitung, Reader's Digest, *The New York Times*, the *New Yorker* and *New York Magazine*.

The commission

This work was commissioned by Patrick de Saint-Exupéry, the editor of the French publication *XXI*. Olivier was asked to complete a 30-page reportage/documentary graphic novel about a person he meets in Iran. The deadline for this brief was very flexible.

3.18

1. The illustrator as artist 2. The medium is the message 3. From outcomes to outlets 4. Communicating ideas 5. Making it happen 6. Production

← Self-initiated illustration   Case study: Olivier Kugler   Try it yourself... →

Initial response

Olivier approached the editor of *XXI* magazine himself and told him that he was going to be travelling to Iran. As a result, he was asked to produce a graphic novel, based on his experiences there. The exact nature of the work and the storyline it would follow was left up to Olivier. After much consideration, Olivier decided to join an Iranian truck driver on a long journey through Iran. He was keen to describe daily life in Iran, as seen from the perspective of the trucker rather than from a tourist's point of view.

The work unfolds

Olivier undertook a four-day trip with truck driver Massih, during which he made rough sketches, wrote down observational notes and took reference photos. When he arrived back in his London studio, he looked through all of the photos and began to make rough thumbnails of the page layouts.

Approval

Although Olivier was not required to seek approval, he did show the editor the work on a regular basis.

Final artwork

The final artwork was created in pencil on A2 (C) paper using the photographs as a reference. When the drawings were complete they were digitally coloured.

Completion

When the work was complete it was reproduced as a 30-page reportage journal in the magazine *XXI* (Autumn edition 2010).

3.18
'A tea in Iran'.
Olivier Kugler
Olivier's work follows the day-to-day life of Iranian truck driver Massih.

Try it yourself...

From outcomes to outlets

In an increasingly visual world, images are constantly vying for our attention. This exercise will allow you to consider how illustrators respond to text and how illustrations are used across many different industries.

Materials

Paper, drawing materials, newspaper/magazine article, a favourite CD, a favourite book.

The brief: Responding to content

Part 1
Find an article from a newspaper or magazine that has been illustrated. Photocopy the article and cut out the original illustration. Respond to the text with a series of thumbnails/rough sketches. Once you have explored a number of solutions, decide which one you feel is most appropriate to the text. Work on this idea so that you have a developed visual rough. Remember to be aware of the dimensions that the image must fit.

Part 2
Select a favourite CD and listen to the tracks. Respond to the music by drawing a series of thumbnails/rough sketches. This initial response may be based on emotion, lyrics, tempo – it is how you respond that is important. Check the dimensions of the CD cover and work on your best idea so that you have a developed rough.

Part 3
Think of a book you have recently read. Respond to the text with a series of thumbnails/rough sketches that you feel evoke the mood of the book. Think about the title and the author, these may be included but you may wish to just create an image – either is fine. Check the dimensions of the book and develop the best idea into a final rough.

These may be completed over a number of different days and you may wish to repeat the exercise. Once you have the three final roughs select one to develop into a final illustration.

Questions in summary

1. Which outlet would you most like to create an illustration for?
2. What qualities are required for each type of final outcome?
3. Which key people would you need to collaborate with for each final outcome?
4. Which areas do your favourite illustrators tend to produce work for?

1. The illustrator as artist 2. The medium is the message 3. From outcomes to outlets 4. Communicating ideas 5. Making it happen 6. Production

← Try it yourself… Questions in summary

Chapter 4 — Communicating ideas

The essence of an illustration is in the thinking – the ideas and concepts that form the backbone of what an image is trying to communicate. Bringing life and a visual form to a text or message is the role of the illustrator – the best in the business combine smart analytical thinking with finely tuned practical skills to create images that have something to say, and the ways and means to say it. Here, we'll take a look at some of the ways to start generating ideas and put them into process.

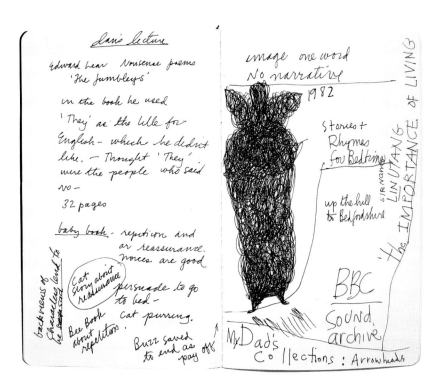

Dan's lecture

Edward Lear — Nonsense poems
'The Jumblies'

in the book he used
'They' as the title for
English — which he didn't
like. — Thought 'They'
were the people who said
no —

32 pages

baby book. repetition and
or reassurance.
noices are good

Cat story about reassurance

persuade to go
to bed —

Bee Book — Cat purring.
about repetition.

Buzz saved
to end as
pay off

back rows of Chevalley lend to he first said

image one word
No narrative
1982

Stories +
Rhymes
for Bedtime

SIR NAME LIN UTANG the IMPORTANCE of LIVING

up the hill
to Bedfordshire

BBC
Sound
archive

My Dad's
Collections : Arrowheads

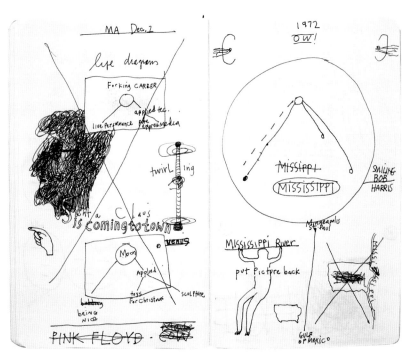

MA Dec. 2

life diagram

Forking CAREER

applied tec.

live Performance pure expression Media

twirl ing

...claus is coming to town

Moon

VENUS

Applied

toys for Christmas

sculpture

being NICE

PINK FLOYD -

1972
OW!

MISSIPPI

MISSISSIPPI

SMILING BOB HARRIS

Minneapolis St. Paul

MISSISSIPPI River

put picture back

GULF of MEXICO

4.1

96

Why ideas?

There is nothing quite so disconcerting as the starkness of a blank sheet of paper or the glare from an empty screen, particularly in between receiving a commission for a professional illustration and making your first mark. In these circumstances, the only satisfactory cure is an idea.

Realizing your idea by putting pencil to paper or finger to mouse is the first step of the journey towards executing an illustration. Understanding how ideas take shape, and how to assist the process when they don't flow as readily as one would like, is crucial if working in illustration is to be a fruitful experience rather than a chore.

Why illustration?

A common misconception amongst student illustrators is that once a 'style' or method of working has been arrived at, there is little more to learn about the craft of illustration. Of course, technique and skills are absolutely invaluable, as is having an approach that could be considered unique. Yet just as important is the ability to create images that are underpinned by strong creative thinking and that have problem-solving ideas at the heart of the solution.

Illustration at its worst is merely a page-filler that might look good, but fails to give any knowledge of the subject that it illustrates. At its best, illustration encourages the viewer to think, to draw more from the text than first meets the eye and to comprehend a greater and more in-depth understanding of the subject. Great illustrations are like great stories and narratives – they require the viewer to become actively involved in order to fully comprehend the message. The concept may appear hidden at first, but communicates successfully when the viewer disseminates the image. Great illustration marries excellence in craft, skill and creative thinking.

1. The illustrator as artist   2. The medium is the message   3. From outcomes to outlets   **4. Communicating ideas**   5. Making it happen   6. Production

Why ideas?   The briefing →

4.1
Sketchbook spreads.
Margaret Huber
Generating ideas is essential as an immediate response to a brief. Many illustrators use their sketchbooks as a place to initiate ideas without constraint.

4.2
Sketchbook spreads.
Sarah Jennings
A unique relationship can develop between the artist/illustrator and their sketchbooks – here is a place where the communication is more personal, where the only audience is the artist themselves, and where pure experimentation with concepts and ideas can begin.

A creative career

Just as trends in fashion or music ebb and flow, so too do styles in illustration. An illustrator recognized for a particular way of working may have a fantastically busy year professionally, only to find that as the commissions start to dry up, their style has fallen out of fashion. Keeping abreast of changes stylistically can help the illustrator stay one step ahead of the competition. However, creating images that resonate with creative ideas helps to produce a body of work that is timeless and doesn't rely on the whims of fashion in design and illustration.

Planning a career in illustration is anything but an exact science and there are no guarantees of longevity. However, many of the illustrators that have survived the test of time, working across a number of decades as opposed to just a number of years, have produced images that require more than just a passing glance from the viewer. Combining strong ideas with excellent execution can ensure an audience continues to appreciate the work of an illustrator, long after fashions and trends have moved on.

'Creating images that resonate with creative ideas helps to produce a body of work that is timeless and doesn't rely on the whims of fashion in design and illustration.'

**AUTHOR TIP:
INVESTIGATING IDEAS**

— Use a sketchbook to record ideas and thoughts in an intuitive and automatic fashion – don't worry about how the ideas look at this stage.
— Carry a sketchbook and pen or pencil at all times – inspiration can occur in the unlikeliest of places so it pays to be prepared.
— Jot down your thoughts using written as well as visual language, whichever best suits your way of thinking.
— Put down enough information to remind you of ideas months, or even years ahead.
— Date and time your entries – this will help you to remember the context of what you were thinking at the time.
— Make a note of locations, reference materials and book titles as well as writing down important quotes that might help.

1. The illustrator as artist   2. The medium is the message   3. From outcomes to outlets   **4. Communicating ideas**   5. Making it happen   6. Production

Why ideas?   The briefing →

BRIEF: Horoscope
'Cancer'

need visual reference

- full colour
- final size 125 × 125 mm
- rough required by end of week (b+w) (indicate colours if poss)
- to be used for calendar
- must feature crab

4.3

Square format

fill space.

if not simplified won't fit format... like idea of crab in water

Simplify image, show 6 legs + claws

like orange on blue (water)

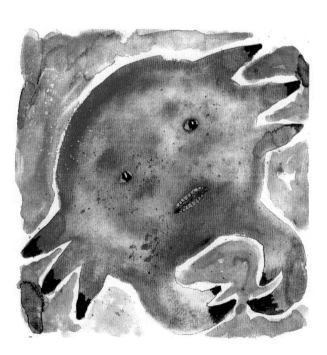

The briefing

Mastering the ability to think creatively should not be shrouded in mystery. With some useful tips, most creative people can lay the foundations to ensure that they are best prepared to be creative in their thinking and start to generate interesting ideas. For the illustrator, the most important aspect of creative thinking starts with the briefing of a new project.

Information gathering

The initial briefing is the point at which basic information about the project must be gathered. Knowledge and understanding of the project is crucial. Being equipped with all of the relevant information required may appear obvious, but many fail to fully comprehend the importance of getting the facts correct at the start.

Knowing where the finished illustration is to appear, at what size, and whether it is to run in colour or black and white, should be basic aspects of the brief – if in doubt, ask. Being fully aware of the deadline for visuals and how much time is then available to complete the final artwork is crucial. If the work is for a new client – understanding the audience and researching previous copies of the publication can help build a picture of how your work may fit in and the range of illustration styles that the publication has used before.

4.3
Horoscope sketches and illustration.
Louise Fenton
Gathering information when receiving a brief is essential. Always ensure that you have the details of the size of the final piece, the content and the deadline and gather visual references. This all feeds into the final piece.

The briefing meeting

Where possible, it is advisable to meet face-to-face with a client to receive a project brief, although this is often not realistic. Most briefings take place on the phone, via email or through agents. Unless the project is of a substantial size, a meeting of real people in real time is unlikely. For those rare face-to-face meetings it is vital to ensure that every aspect of a project is covered in detail. It is in these very early beginnings of a project that initial ideas can start to take shape.

The possible meeting and associated conversation should act as a catalyst for the exploration of ideas. To ensure it is successful, be aware of the need to listen. Listening to the client talk about the project will help shape the direction of your visual solutions. Don't be afraid to ask questions, but then do make sure that you listen to the answers. No question that you ask will be inappropriate – you can never have too much information.

If you find that the client talks about the project in language that you don't comprehend, or in jargon that doesn't make sense – make sure that you ask them to rephrase what they are saying. Write down key points, but don't let your attention to writing stop you from listening. Clarify points later if you need to, but at this stage just get the broad brushstroke of the project.

When you leave the meeting or put down the phone, start by putting as much of the information you've been given on to paper as soon as possible. Write down every detail, every thought, idea and concept – however random, basic or crazy they may seem at the time. These notes will prove invaluable later as they will have been created from the fresh thoughts and instinctive responses you had to the project in the first instance.

Being armed with the facts can make a big difference – it makes sense to start generating ideas fortified with as much information as possible.

1. The illustrator as artist   2. The medium is the message   3. From outcomes to outlets   4. Communicating ideas   5. Making it happen   6. Production

← Why ideas?   The briefing   Investigating the subject matter →

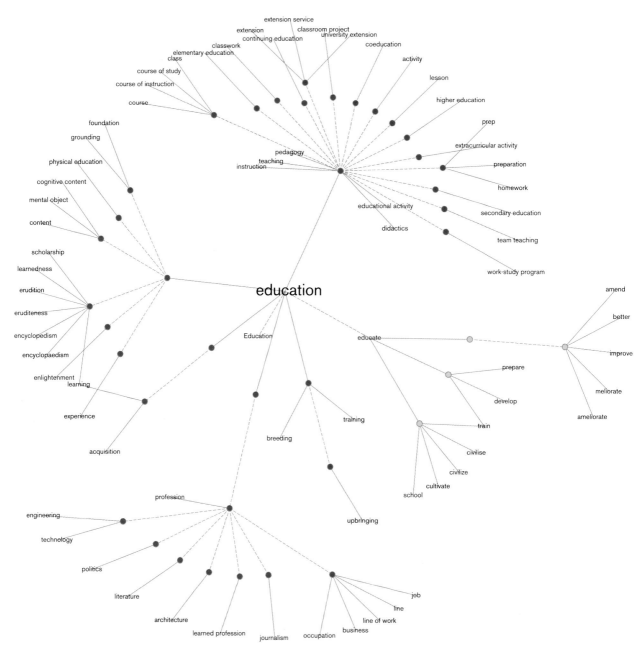

extension service
extension
classroom project
continuing education
university extension
classwork
elementary education
coeducation
class
activity
course of study
lesson
course of instruction
higher education
course
prep
foundation
extracurricular activity
grounding
preparation
physical education
pedagogy
homework
cognitive content
teaching
instruction
secondary education
mental object
team teaching
content
educational activity
work-study program
didactics
scholarship
learnedness
amend
erudition
better
eruditeness
encyclopedism
improve
encyclopaedism
education
enlightenment
learning
educate
experience
Education
prepare
meliorate
acquisition
develop
ameliorate
breeding
training
train
civilise
profession
civilize
engineering
cultivate
technology
school
upbringing
politics
literature
job
architecture
line
learned profession
line of work
journalism
business
occupation

4.4
Visual thesaurus.
There are a number of ways
to generate ideas and identify
associated words. This diagram
shows cycles of words that relate
to each other and is visually more
stimulating than writing a list.

Investigating the subject matter

The illustrator frequently begins a project having been emailed text or copy from their client. This is particularly true for newspaper, magazine or book publishing commissions. A newspaper may have a regular IT feature or health page that requires illustrating, or a magazine may commission illustrators to produce images to accompany the text of their regular columnists.

Whatever the type of commission, it is wise to investigate the subject matter of the text in as much depth as possible. Researching on the Internet, and in bookshops and libraries, should harvest more information than the text for the magazine or newspaper article can possibly cover. Having more information about the subject can throw new light on to possible avenues of thought.

It is useful to build a bigger picture, but don't forget the original text. Get as much information as you can – obviously, the most important thing at the start of a project is to understand the subject that you are illustrating. Be careful though, remember that you are being commissioned to create an illustration that complements the text being published.

Getting started

When an illustrator is busy with numerous commissions the greatest temptation is to place any new incoming projects to the bottom of the pile and ignore them until the impending deadline looms so close that it becomes impossible to put off the project any longer. For many freelance illustrators there is an in-built aversion to completing a job before the specified deadline. This is not due to laziness, but the fear of being without work. Being freelance means that there are times when one is busy and other times when one is without work, or 'in-between projects', as actors like to describe unemployment. Having a backlog of work maintains the sense of full employment. This process of leaving projects until the very last minute is not conducive to creative thinking, though.

It is wise to get to grips with a project as soon as possible. Often the best ideas will come when least expected – in the shower, on the bus, whilst cooking – but this can only happen if the project has been investigated, or at least the text has been digested, early on. Reading the text through thoroughly a few times in a quiet space, with a cup of coffee and a notepad and pen handy is the ideal way to start the creative process. Printing a second copy of the text and having it to hand in a bag with a notepad and pen, so that it can be called upon and referred to whenever there is a free moment makes real sense. Remember that a good idea can take shape anywhere.

1. The illustrator as artist   2. The medium is the message   3. From outcomes to outlets   4. Communicating ideas   5. Making it happen   6. Production

← The briefing   Investigating the subject matter   Gathering inspiration →

> **AUTHOR TIP:**
> **RESEARCH AND IDEAS SHEETS**
>
> — Collect words – use a written list to itemise everything that you can think of that is connected to the project. Use a highlighter pen to mark those words that seem potent and that may add something to your thinking.
> — Cut up your lists and place the chosen words onto a fresh sheet of paper; tape them down and start to draw lines between words where you see possible links. Look for themes – both in thinking and in visual terms. New words and visuals will start to form – create them, write them down and add these to your diagram. Go down unexplored routes and see what happens – be spontaneous.

Starting the process early on and filling the brain with as much related information about the subject matter as possible will kick-start the process of ideas generation. Try to be relaxed and have the confidence to recognize that good creative ideas can take time to form. Training the mind not to panic in the face of slow developments is a key aspect of the creative process. In essence, don't arrive at the blank sheet of paper or screen in an unprepared state – read the brief, understand your audience and arrive armed with your notes.

Making notes

Everyone has a different approach to making notes. Some like to scribble single words and phrases, others prefer to write their thoughts out in long hand, while others create a combination of sketches, and handwritten thoughts and explanations. Find the method that best suits your own purposes – use a sketchbook, or a notebook, sheets of copier paper, write onto the printed brief itself, whichever method feels right.

Start by reading the brief or the text all the way through, as well as the notes that you made at the briefing meeting if it occurred, without trying to make notes. Of course, if ideas or thoughts spring to mind during this first read-through, get them briefly down on paper, but use it primarily simply as an opportunity to gain an understanding of the story or article. It is very unlikely that you'll know nothing about the content of the text; the art director commissioning the illustration will have mentioned something of the content on the phone or in an email when asking if you would like to take on the commission.

Make sure that your interpretation of the text is clear – it may differ from the original thoughts you had about the project before you had a chance to read it. This is quite normal, so it is always best to delay making any decisions about your illustration, however small, until you have read the text thoroughly.

During a second or third reading, start to make notes. Don't worry about the shape that they take – these notes are not for an external audience, but will be useful reminders and pointers when you look back at them. Make sure that you understand your own notes – you may not return to them for a few days and they need to be easily referenced and used. Use a highlighter pen to underline key areas of text – there will often be useful sections that summarize the overall points that the writer is making. Some illustrators find it useful to staple blank sheets of paper in between the sheets of text to jot notes and ideas on to.

The note-taking stage is purely to establish initial thoughts and the beginnings of connections and ideas. Don't panic if, during the first session, you find that nothing concrete has emerged. You will have fed through much information contained within the text and your mind will use this over the course of the following hours or, ideally, days.

**AUTHOR TIP:
MOODBOARDS**

— Some illustrators like to start a project by creating a moodboard from sketches and collected ephemera. This approach is determined by the kind of project that has been commissioned. If a set of images is being produced, moodboards can reflect the overall visual style of the work.
— Moodboards may represent colours, shapes, tones and textures, but can also be used to group visual objects and to set the scene of the artwork. They can be useful reference points for the illustrator and act as excellent visual guides for clients too.
— Start a moodboard by collecting and visualizing potential aspects and tape or tack them onto sheets of paper or board – foam board is useful for this, being lightweight yet rigid. Having your moodboard in front of you whilst working can assist the process too, providing a constant reference point.

First visual representation

The notes you have created are probably just single words or phrases, and perhaps a few key sentences. You may have also produced some very simple visuals. These visuals are unlikely to be anything more than scribbles, a visual form of note-taking, characterized by the simplicity of the line – a figure represented by a stick man, a building by a child-like drawing of a house, for example. Recognize these drawings as the first stages towards visualizing written language – they may not hold the key to producing the final illustration, but they are the stepping stones or building blocks towards later illustrations. Get into the habit of working this way – some find it easier than taking written notes – but just as in writing, ensure that you get enough detail down to remember exactly what the point of the drawings was.

'Recognize these drawings as the first stages towards visualizing written language.'

1. The illustrator as artist   2. The medium is the message   3. From outcomes to outlets   4. Communicating ideas   5. Making it happen   6. Production

← The briefing   Investigating the subject matter   Gathering inspiration →

4.5

4.5
Google image searches
For many, a Google image search can be the first step in visual research.

Gathering inspiration

Inspiration for projects and for the ideas that drive projects will not come from just researching the subject in hand. An illustrator must constantly be on the look out for inspiration and reference materials and resources. Most illustrators create their own archives of images and objects, organizing their collections into folders, drawers and boxes. These collections can be incredible sources of inspiration.

The action of constantly looking and recording is very much part of the illustrator's lifestyle. Inspiration is everywhere, a cliché perhaps, but so very true. Finding time to dive into a second-hand bookshop or car boot sale, photographing a moment or mood, capturing a sentence uttered by a stranger overheard in a supermarket – these can all be inspirational and deserve their own space in an illustrator's archives.

It may be a simple combination of colours used in a piece of packaging, the way a figure is captured in a photograph or the texture of a used tram ticket from a childhood vacation that inspires – there is a sixth sense that illustrators develop when collecting and collating reference materials.

Setting up an archive of reference materials is an enjoyable process and although it can be time-consuming, it is a thoroughly worthwhile and useful aspect of the creative process. Being aware of your influences, and of the visual aesthetics that you respond well to, will lead successfully to gaining inspiration and ideas from the everyday.

4.6
American sketchbook.
Howard Read
Here, drawings were made, printed ephemera gathered and notes written to document a trip across America on public transport.

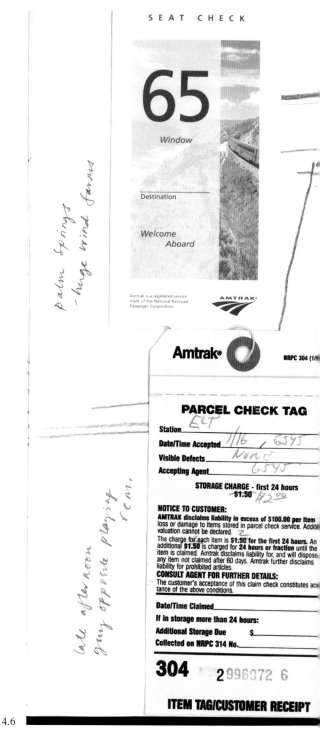

4.6

1. The illustrator as artist   2. The medium is the message   3. From outcomes to outlets   **4. Communicating ideas**   5. Making it happen   6. Production

← Investigating the subject matter   Gathering inspiration   Brainstorming →

The sketchbook

A sketchbook is the illustrator's best friend. A sketchbook is not just for sketching and drawing in though, it should be a constant companion and the one item that the illustrator turns to to record and document notes, found images and all manner of inspirational material. Get into the habit of carrying it with you at all times, buy one that fits in your pocket or in a bag that you always use. Don't make the mistake of replacing your sketchbook with a diary or a time-planner – they are different things. You should not have to schedule time to be creative, it should just occur, and when it does you need to be prepared.

Use your sketchbook to record everything, don't worry about keeping it specifically for either personal or professional work – put everything in and you'll find that the two areas mix and merge. Draw, doodle, write and take notes whenever and wherever possible. Clip out findings from newspapers and magazines and tape them in, staple in ticket stubs and any kind of ephemera that you've found or collected. Stick in photographs, rescued pieces of photocopied images, stencils, stickers, flyers, cards… the list is endless.

The project file

A file created for each project is another method of storing all related materials, ideas and inspirations as well as the formal paperwork relating to a project such as the brief, the contract and reference material supplied by the client. It is useful to create both a digital and analogue project file. Creating a new folder, saved on to your hard disk for all correspondence, copies of emails, and digital reference material is as important as a real-world version. Like an expanded and more focused version of the sketchbook, the project file can encompass everything that relates to, or that could relate to, the project in hand.

A useful project file is one that houses every aspect of the project – from relevant pages torn from sketchbooks to a series of photographic reference images, and photocopies from second-hand books to print-outs from Google searches. It is this material that will assist in inspiring ideas – spread out all of your reference materials, notes and written and visual research in front of you whilst you work. The blank sheet of paper or screen will feel less daunting when surrounded by the visual material that has fed into your thinking.

4.7
'Mechanical hedgehog'.
Pencil drawings in an old novel.
Matt Jones
Collect everything in
sketchbooks: drawings, notes,
doodles, photographs, stencils,
stickers, clippings…

The creative environment

Working in a positive environment can do wonders for the generation of creative ideas. Finding a calm, quiet space to retreat to works for most people. Turning phones off and quitting an email application will all help to ensure that your time is not interrupted by a constant flow of communication from the outside world.

Organizing a work space, clearing the digital desktop and cleaning the real-world desktop all help in metaphorically freeing up some fresh space in which to think. Empty the studio bin, open a window and let in some fresh air – make your environment fresh and it will help you reap the rewards.

Some people not only clean and clear, they also re-jig their work spaces at the start of a new project. They reposition their screen, tidy the spaghetti chaos of their computer cables and reorganize their bookcases. Archiving previous projects, or filing papers away into their relevant folders can be a real plus too, mentally helping to bring a conclusion to finished work before the fresh start of a brand new project.

Whilst many like to make a hot drink to relax with as they start the thinking process, plenty of others find creative realization can come from actually leaving the studio environment and having a drink in a local coffee shop or café. There is something unique about sitting with a new project on the table with a pen in one hand and a frothy cappuccino in the other. Being away from normal distractions and focusing the mind on the job in hand can be hugely beneficial.

The more time that you spend working as an illustrator the more you can begin to recognize and then concentrate on the particular ways that best suit your approach to creative thinking. Learn to capitalize on the scenarios and locations that work most effectively for you. If your best ideas come during the afternoon, learn from this and use your mornings to work at other aspects of illustration, such as filing, emailing, invoicing and marketing.

Know the point when it is best that you walk away from the process of creating ideas; learn to accept when your creative juices are not flowing. Hitting a brick wall or a black hole – call a creative block what you like – is not fun, but it does happen to all of us and on a regular basis too. Banging your head against that wall will not help – getting out for a walk in the fresh air, wandering around an exhibition or catching a movie may be all you need to clear the mind and prepare yourself for another attempt. Knowing when to stop is as vital as knowing how to start.

**AUTHOR TIP:
CONNECTIONS**

— Allow yourself to explore connections – it may be that seemingly unconnected words or visuals, once brought together, bring a new meaning or start a chain of other connections. Just the juxtaposition of two or three elements can lead an idea in a new direction – don't be afraid to experiment.
— Many illustrators use metaphors successfully in their work. A metaphor can be a word or image that isn't to be read or viewed literally, but makes a comparison. Using symbolism or figures of speech that do not represent real things can be described as a metaphor.
— Words and word play can provide starting points as well as solutions for the illustrator looking to create visuals with grounding in language. An old-fashioned thesaurus will work just as well as an online version.
— Spider diagrams can be particularly useful when working with a complex set of problems or with information less easy to visually define. Start by making notes about the range of subjects or headings that you wish to investigate and then add further notes and research about each as you work through them.

1. The illustrator as artist   2. The medium is the message   3. From outcomes to outlets   **4. Communicating ideas**   5. Making it happen   6. Production

← Investigating the subject matter   Gathering inspiration   Brainstorming →

4.8
Initial sketches for
'My East End'.
Jason Ford
Early rough sketches identify a
stylistic approach and aspects of
the subject matter. These drawings
are quick studies and a method for
generating ideas through visual
exploration. Nothing is decided or
rejected at this stage – everything
still counts.

Brainstorming

Once in possession of a fully formed project brief, notes and interpretations from the briefing meeting, a sketchbook with early inspirations and thoughts, research into the subject area as well as a project file and a fully functioning creative environment to work in, it's time to start formulating some ideas!

Brainstorming can mean different things to different people. Simply expressed, it is the action of bringing together all of the research, notes, scribbles and thoughts and creating a series of bigger and more clearly defined ideas and paths to follow. Illustrators, unlike designers, will often have to brainstorm alone – illustration can be a lonely pursuit; as a solo activity there is only one person responsible for the final outcome. Of course, working with an art director or designer on a project can help, and discussing ideas should be very much part of the process, but ultimately there is only one person creating the initial ideas – you, the illustrator.

An onslaught of ideas and thoughts is the best way to describe how brainstorming should work. Get every idea and thought out and onto paper or screen. Keep your ideas flowing – good ideas, bad ideas, exciting, dull – let them all out. Just like a storm of heavy rain and gusting wind, your brain should be working overtime to produce as much as it can. Examine possibilities, explore links, twist meanings and subvert thoughts – anything goes. To make brainstorming work, you need to have the germs of ideas and lots of them.

1. The illustrator as artist 2. The medium is the message 3. From outcomes to outlets **4. Communicating ideas** 5. Making it happen 6. Production

← Gathering inspiration Brainstorming Explaining the visual →

4.8

AUTHOR TIP:
HISTORICAL RESEARCH

— Historical accuracy may not be a factor in most illustrations, but whenever a project calls for detailed visual information about a subject, it is wise to undertake some in-depth research.
— Using expert information from reliable sources will ensure that mistakes are not made.

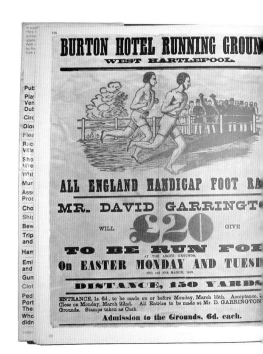

4.9
Inspiration for 'My East End'.
These are some of the books used as
reference by Jason Ford while working
on illustrations to accompany a short
story set in Victorian London.

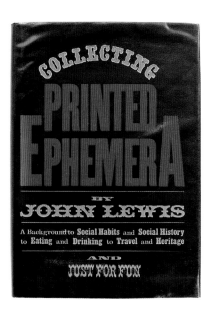

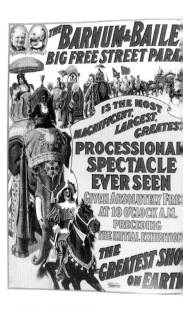

1. The illustrator as artist 2. The medium is the message 3. From outcomes to outlets **4. Communicating ideas** 5. Making it happen 6. Production

← Gathering inspiration Brainstorming Explaining the visual →

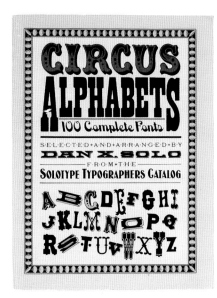

The investigation of ideas

There are numerous ways that ideas can take shape after the initial brainstorming exercise. Recognizing how to use the raw materials of creative thinking is the next stage in the process. Evaluating and editing your ideas can be just as difficult as the conception. Recognizing a strong idea and working it through to a conclusion or following a thread of creative thinking to the next logical stage are all aspects of the process that improve with practice.

Embracing both a sense of realism – the image must communicate a message after all – and maintaining a high level of creativity can help translate the results of brainstorming into fully formed concepts. Being realistic means that the wildest, most bizarre and unreadable ideas are kept away from production. Reminding yourself that the work must communicate is about being realistic. On the other hand, being creative means that the work stays fresh, takes risks and feels edgy – you are an artist after all. The right measure of realism and creativity is the goal.

Investigating your ideas and moving them into more concrete forms relies on a variety of means. Looking for connections, bringing words and images together or juxtaposing a number of elements can lead ideas in new directions. Viewing your concepts from an opposing angle can help, too – a new perspective on the problem can be a fresh start. The use of colour can affect the mood of the image, whilst using metaphors can shift the emphasis of an idea or concept.

4.10
Initial compositions for 'My East End'.
Jason Ford
The next stage in developing the illustration is to work with the independently created elements and visuals from the sketch stage to build up a range of test compositions. It helps to give your compositions a space to occupy – a simple rectangular line around the image shows the edge of the page or the image. Cropping into particular details can provide a more dynamic focus – practise this with two L-shaped pieces of card to frame different aspects of your work.

Risk-taking in illustration

The term 'risk' implies danger. Let's face it though – to the outside world the very idea that illustrators face risks and dangers on a daily basis is a little preposterous. Where risk-taking does come into effect in illustration is at the point where safe ideas and routes into a project are jettisoned in favour of a less tried and tested route.

Opening new doors into the unknown and facing creative problems head-on without the safety net of familiarity is about being brave. Flying in the face of conformity and tackling problems within projects with new thinking and, at times, new ways of making images can be the essence of what moves an illustrator's work forward – staving off the staleness of repetition.

Taking risks is a necessary aspect of creative thinking as well as in image-making itself. The future of an illustrator's career and the future of the discipline, rest on constantly moving forward and exploring new avenues of thinking.

A stale illustrator will produce stale images. Often the greatest enemy of fresh original thinking is not the client, but the illustrator themselves. Having fallen into a formulaic 'style' of work, their approach to ideas generation and thinking relies too heavily on clichés without pushing into cleverer and more challenging areas. It is wise to recognize the symptoms and work hard to ensure – through constant exposure to new materials, reference and research – that making illustrations remains a challenge.

Only through stepping into uncharted territories can new discoveries be made that will ultimately take one's work forward. On occasion, taking risks can lead to frustrations as not every attempt will come to fruition. Learning to recognize the pitfalls as well as the rewards is the first stage in facing the challenge, however.

1. The illustrator as artist   2. The medium is the message   3. From outcomes to outlets   **4. Communicating ideas**   5. Making it happen   6. Production

← Gathering inspiration   Brainstorming   Explaining the visual →

Ideas into visuals and roughs

It is one thing to get through the stages of ideas-generation intact and find a level of thinking and visual representation that you feel happy is solving the project brief. It is another stage of work to ensure that your client, and often their client, is as keen on your approach and has as much faith in the work as you do.

It is extremely rare to be given complete freedom with a project, or be allowed to rush straight into creating finished artwork without supplying visuals that describe your thinking and the route that you'll be taking to construct that final artwork.

A visual or 'rough', as it is sometimes called, should ideally be a sketch that demonstrates loosely the elements that will appear in the work, although nothing will be completed in any great detail at this stage. Unfortunately, the ideal is now becoming threatened as commissioners have started to expect visuals with more and more detail explored. This may be a reaction to the number of illustrators now creating images on screen. Clients can and will demand changes because they believe that the work can be modified by the illustrator easily on a computer. Expectations of more polished and finished visuals have been led by the growth in digital hardware and software – the equipment has created a culture where perfection is now a given.

4.11
Adding colour to initial sketches for 'My East End'.
Jason Ford
Initial sketches were worked up in Photoshop and coloured for two versions. Note how the use of light and shade on the clouds gives the image a greater depth and sense of perspective.

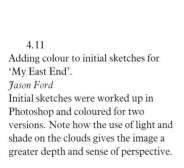

4.11

'A visual or "rough", as it is sometimes called, should ideally be a sketch that demonstrates loosely the elements that will appear in the work.'

1. The illustrator as artist 2. The medium is the message 3. From outcomes to outlets **4. Communicating ideas** 5. Making it happen 6. Production

← Gathering inspiration Brainstorming Explaining the visual →

Explaining the visual

More often than not, once a set of ideas has been fine-tuned into a definitive route forward, the visual will be emailed to the client for consideration. Obviously with bigger projects, a face-to-face meeting may well be set up, but 95 per cent of all visuals will arrive without the benefit of a verbal explanation as accompaniment. Sending a visual via email without any text explaining the route that you have taken with the brief can easily result in a negative response to your work. This will not always happen, but why take that risk? Courtesy, if nothing else, determines that it is a good idea to explain what your client is looking at.

Write a simple and concise explanation of the work, summarizing your thinking, and detail what will change in the process of moving from visual to final artwork. Make reference to colours and textures that may change and note where elements will require further work – perhaps more detailed drawing will be required in some areas, for example. Keep the commissioner in the loop by explaining your thinking and ideas a little. Highlight the key elements in the brief that you felt required exploring and expanding upon. Remember your client – the designer, art director or art buyer – is likely to have to present your visual to someone else too. It may go to an editor or a more senior creative director and it may have to be shown to a client that is not as visually aware as the designer that you are working with. If you are working on an advertising campaign, for example, your work may be presented to a team from the company that the advertising agency is working for. They could be the marketing department from a shoe or a washing detergent manufacturers – not necessarily the ideal audience to comprehend a rough visual working of an idea!

4.12
Client approval for 'My East End'.
Jason Ford
Even at what appears to be a late stage in this project, the client requested changes, wanting the image to have a more modern, upbeat and comical feel. Further black-and-white sketches were produced and shown to the client before commencing the final artwork. The final piece certainly has a more engaging feel, but still reflects the research and investigation conducted earlier.

AUTHOR TIP:
EXPLORING HOW IMAGES WORK

— Images help an audience perceive an idea and the role of illustration is to bring visual meaning to a given text. Images can be simple, complex, emotional, diagrammatic or documentary. Most importantly, they should aim to present a point of view and they should make the viewer think. Images in the context of illustration should be unique – causing the viewer to see something in a way that they normally would not. They should also be emotional, bringing a sense of humanity to the viewer, as well as being appropriate and understandable.
— Visual communication relies on a mix of signs and symbols – how we 'read' images and how we decode their meanings occurs in a subconscious manner. The 'voice' inherent within an image is translated by an audience that have learnt how to understand and comprehend visual images through associations built up over the years.
— For an illustrator to bring these elements together into one image is no small achievement – all inextricably linked to a creative idea too, of course.

If you do get the opportunity to present your work in person, even at the visuals stage – leap at it. Getting some valuable experience of explaining your work is crucial. Offer to meet with clients if and when you can. Sitting down and talking face-to-face at both a briefing meeting and at the visuals stage can really iron out any slight misinterpretations from either side of the fence.

When speaking about your ideas and visual approach, be confident, speak clearly and use the visual to illustrate your explanations. If you get nervous in meeting situations, make some notes before you arrive – work out what you wish to say and don't be afraid to follow your notes.

Be prepared to talk through your work and to take on board relevant considerations and comments from those looking at your work. Try to react positively to advice and criticism about the work so far. Don't take any criticism of your thinking personally, further work may well be needed to help the illustration solve the brief in a way that the client is happy with. Take notes and be civil, but if you believe that you have valid points – make sure that you voice them: you will be respected for doing so. An illustrator should bring a different viewpoint and perspective to a project – stand up for yourself and have a strong belief in your contribution.

1. The illustrator as artist   2. The medium is the message   3. From outcomes to outlets   **4. Communicating ideas**   5. Making it happen   6. Production

← Brainstorming   Explaining the visual   Case study: Damian Gascoigne →

4.12

Case study: Damian Gascoigne

Damian Gascoigne is a professional animator, filmmaker, illustrator and educator. His animation work has featured in competitions at animation festivals around the world, winning numerous awards and nominations along the way. He divides his time between commercial animation and illustration projects for clients such as McCann Erickson in New York, *The Guardian* newspaper in the UK and WPP Marketing. He has recently been teaching animation at Seoul National University in Korea.

4.13

The client

WPP Marketing, a world leader in marketing communications services.

The commission

Damian was asked to complete 60 illustrations over a three-week period. The commission was to create images for WPP Marketing's website for human resources and training for work-related situations.

Initial response

Starting with rough drawings to generate ideas, Damian created a number of initial sketches. He then identified those that he felt had the most potential. At this stage, he started looking for reference materials in books and on the Internet.

Final artwork

Damian painted his line work in ink and then scanned it into the computer to colour and compose the final artwork. Test images were printed before the final version in order to ensure the best decisions were made with regards to colour and design.

4.13
Final artwork.
Damian Gascoigne
The final images went on to be published on WPP Marketing's website.

1. The illustrator as artist   2. The medium is the message   3. From outcomes to outlets   4. Communicating ideas   5. Making it happen   6. Production

← Explaining the visual   Case study: Damian Gascoigne   Try it yourself... →

Try it yourself...

Communicating ideas

When communicating ideas it is essential to research a number of potential solutions to the brief. This project will help you to explore your own methods of generating ideas, allowing your mind to think freely.

Materials

You don't need masses of materials for the initial response to a brief. A drawing implement and some paper is all that is required. Some illustrators prefer to use layout paper for this initial idea phase, some prefer to use a sketchbook and some just use any scraps of paper that happen to be around. Over time you will develop your own way of working.

The brief: Illustrating a letter

Develop a series of small 'thumbnail' responses to illustrate the first letter of your first name. Start by writing the letter on the paper you will be working on, this will act as a constant reminder of what the brief is.

You should aim to work quickly and draw, write, notate everything that you can think of that begins with the same letter. You might also begin to explore things beyond the letter itself. For example, the letter 'p' might make you think of peas and this might in turn make you think of vegetables – and so the initial idea begins to loosen and your imagination can run wild!

Your aim should be to fill as many small squares as possible. Let your imagination run free and don't worry about visual accuracy. These responses allow you to put every idea down on paper. Your initial response is important: you never know, the ideas may be revisited in the future.

Aim to spend no more than 90 minutes on this. By restricting your time, you have to focus on the brief and your mind will not have time to wander.

Questions in summary

1. How can ideas be generated and recorded?
2. What basic information about a project should be gathered before work can begin?
3. How might an illustrator start to explore in more detail the initial ideas for a project?
4. Where might an illustrator look for inspiration?
5. Why is it important to be able to explain your work to a client?
6. How can an illustrator help to ensure that their work is unique, appropriate and long-lasting?

1. The illustrator as artist   2. The medium is the message   3. From outcomes to outlets   **4. Communicating ideas**   5. Making it happen   6. Production

← Try it yourself…   Questions in summary

Chapter 5 — Making it happen

Unlike graphic design, there is not a clearly visible, tried-and-tested path into working as a freelance illustrator. Forging a career can take equal amounts of patience, skill and luck. Understanding how to market one's work, maintain client interest and build a professional reputation can be a painstaking experience.

5.1

Marketing the product and the art of self-promotion

It is quite possible that some of the very best illustration currently being created will never see the light of day. It will never leave the screen or the portfolio of the person creating it, as they are unable or unwilling to engage in promoting their work. Being able to market, promote and generally inform the illustration commissioners of your work is as vital to working in the field as the ability to create an image in the first place. Without a marketing campaign, even a very simple one, an illustrator can fall at the first hurdle.

As covered in the previous chapters, there are many different aspects and areas to the world of design, advertising and communication. Each offers opportunities for illustrators to win commissions and create work; the secret is in understanding how to make that first point of contact and then maintain the interest in your work throughout your career.

When mid-sized and large corporate companies want to extend their market share and increase sales they promote themselves. They will hire a PR company or an advertising agency, use broadcast media, create print and publishing campaigns and experiment with outdoor and indoor media. For the lone illustrator, the budget for promotion may be dramatically smaller, but the intentions are very similar.

The right audience

The key to positive promotion is to ensure that all communication is aimed squarely at the intended audience. Therefore, forming an up-to-date list of potential clients is as important as creating positive and worthwhile self-promotional material. The type of list can vary from illustrator to illustrator; some would class a little black book of phone numbers and contact addresses as a definitive and exhaustive resource. Others, however, would claim that a database software application that merges contact details, can be utilized to email specific groups, as well as to print selected entries on to labels for mail-shot purposes, is far more useful.

The design, publishing and advertising worlds are different from other types of industry in that it is rare for people to stay in the same job for much more than a year or two, compared to five years elsewhere. Finding out who is working with whom and at which company can take time. Even after completing a list of art directors working on magazines in New York, for instance, many will have moved jobs, gone elsewhere or moved up the ladder.

Successful illustrators who choose to represent themselves may spend an entire day a week updating mailing lists and databases, initiating meetings and sending out cards and samples, just to stay ahead of the pack. This process can be mundane and difficult to maintain when busy with work, but it is crucial to ensure a constant flow of commissions.

1. The illustrator as artist   2. The medium is the message   3. From outcomes to outlets   4. Communicating ideas   5. Making it happen   6. Production

Marketing the product and the art of self-promotion   Portfolios →

5.1
'Haberdashery', giclée print created for an exhibition and shown alongside the work of Steven Lenton.
Mia Nilsson
Exhibitions are just one of a number of opportunities for self-promotion.

Contact databases

It is possible to beat the drudgery of compiling lists of names, titles, addresses, phone, fax, email and Web details by using the increasing number of information and contact companies that exist. They will supply ready-to-use databases of creative industry employee details on CD or via email.

Although these services are not vastly expensive, for the lone illustrator starting out in the business the costs may be prohibitive. One approach can be to purchase one list at a time rather than hoping to hit all areas of the industry in the same marketing exercise. Often these companies produce separate lists for each of the design, book, newspaper and magazine publishing and advertising industries, and these can be purchased separately. It is worth remembering that each database will have a best-before date of six months; most suppliers update their records every three months. A glance at the classified ads in the back pages of most prominent design and advertising magazines will detail any companies supplying contact information.

Cold-calling – making telephone calls to potential clients on the off-chance that they may have work or want to view a portfolio – is rarely successful. There was a time when magazine art directors and design company creative directors would put aside an afternoon each week to view portfolios and meet with freelance illustrators and photographers. Unfortunately, this magical slot appears to have disappeared in recent years, partly due to increased workloads, but also because other forms of self-promotion have become popular. Clients, after the initial contact has been made, are happy to converse on the phone, via email and to view images on screen from attachments or websites, so for many the face-to-face meeting has become a thing of the past.

Targeting

Promotional material arriving on the desk of the right person is just one aspect of the self-promotion process. Ensuring that the most appropriate companies and organizations are targeted in the first place takes research and investigation. Understanding where, within the industry, your work will best fit is also important. There is little point in costly marketing to design companies specializing in corporate annual reports if you are a children's book illustrator, for example.

Research

Regular, straightforward research into potential clients can be done on a weekly or monthly basis without huge inconvenience or expense. Keeping abreast of industry news and changes can be enjoyable, as well as productive. Visit a good library to read the wide range of monthly design and advertising press for information about specific commissions, as well as current projects being undertaken. This is the perfect way of gaining a broad knowledge of current industry trends. It is also possible to compile lists of art directors and designers working in magazines and newspapers from the information reproduced in publications.

5.2

1. The illustrator as artist   2. The medium is the message   3. From outcomes to outlets   4. Communicating ideas   **5. Making it happen**   6. Production

Marketing the product and the art of self-promotion   Portfolios →

5.2
'Crocodile', self-promotional piece.
Damian Gascoigne
Promotional material arriving
on the desk of the right person at
the right time is just part of the
marketing process!

5.3

5.3
'Mermaid', self-promotional
postcard.
Jack Taylor
Self-promotional work such as this
can help to get illustrators known
and recognized.

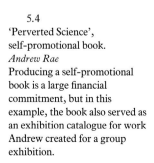

5.4
'Perverted Science',
self-promotional book.
Andrew Rae
Producing a self-promotional
book is a large financial
commitment, but in this
example, the book also served as
an exhibition catalogue for work
Andrew created for a group
exhibition.

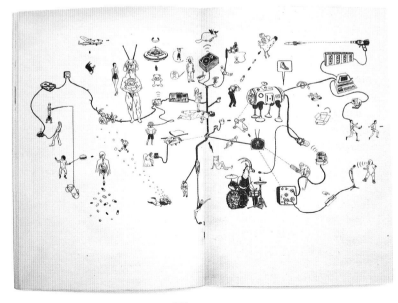

Mail-shots

Making the first contact with a potential client is important and creating the right impression is vital; the professional approach is to create a mail-shot that is simply posted to the recipient. Knowing what to send and how to package it is paramount to your mail-shot's success.

Postcards

Traditionally, illustrators produce postcards as samples of their work. They are relatively inexpensive to produce, cheap to send, and art directors and designers often have filing systems to accommodate them for future reference. Postcards are normally A6 (4.13in x 5.83in) in size, but a double-sized A5 (5.83in x 8.27in) card can look more professional. There are a vast number of print companies that have tapped into the market for producing postcards, many working exclusively for freelance photographers, models, actors and illustrators. Their rates can be reasonable as they 'gang up' the artwork, printing entire sheets of cards and not beginning production and print until they have collected enough artwork to fill the sheet.

Results can vary; some print companies will only supply a digital colour proof that will not give any information about the quality of the colour-match between the artwork and the final print. You tend to get what you pay for.

A successful way of creating well-printed cards on a good stock is to set up a group of illustrators and photographers – enough for an entire sheet – and approach independent printers with the job. Remember it will increase the workload for the person charged with coordinating artwork, payments, preparing the digital files for the printer and ensuring that the deadline for delivery from each of the individual artists is met. Many illustration groups or collectives operate their own print programme to enable a steady and regular update of their printed publicity in exactly this manner.

Printed promos

Postcards can leave some illustrators cold, believing that as creative individuals they should produce promotional materials in line with this – something more personal and memorable. It is true that other formats may interest and intrigue the viewer, but the life expectancy of the piece should be questioned. If it is too large to file with postcards, or to stick on a wall or notice board, or if it is expected to take up valuable desk space, it is likely to be kept just hours rather than months. Every morning of every working day designers and art directors open their post, which mostly contains promotional materials from freelance creatives, and they make snap decisions about what to keep and what to bin.

If promotional material is to be effective, it must grab the viewer's attention and present the facts and contact information in a clear, but interesting manner.

e-marketing

Many illustrators now prefer to send mail-shots electronically. These work in much the same way as their printed counterparts but can be quicker, cheaper and easier to circulate. The downside, of course, is that they can be easily forgotten or 'trashed'!

1. The illustrator as artist   2. The medium is the message   3. From outcomes to outlets   4. Communicating ideas   5. Making it happen   6. Production

Marketing the product and the art of self-promotion   Portfolios →

Portfolios

Without a portfolio of work, the best publicity mail-out will be a wasted opportunity. The portfolio is the single most important asset that an illustrator needs to invest time, energy, attention to detail and finances in. Without a great portfolio working to your advantage, the next commission will be a long wait.

A portfolio may appear to be simply a selection of work in a binder of some description, but that assumption could cost an illustrator a dream project. To say that illustrators live and die by the strength of their portfolio is not an exaggeration. Whether tucked under your arm or tucked away on the Web, a great portfolio is essential.

Analogue portfolios

Even in this digital age, real-world, real-time portfolios are still at the core of self-promotion.

Buying guide

The first rule is to invest money in something that works well and looks the part. Using a battered plastic folio is fine if you are a student ferrying work back and forth from your room to art school. If you wish to be taken seriously, however, and aim to compete with the bigger fish, then you need to give your work the best possible presentation.

All good graphic-art material suppliers stock a range of products that will fit any budget, but spending money here is a good investment. A zipped, leather, ring-bound or loose-leaf book with perfectly clear translucent sleeves is not cheap, but it will stand the test of time and it will perform in an admirable fashion on your behalf. A good comfortable handle is important, as is a place to put your contact details on the outside of the book. A ring-bound book with sleeves will grow with you and adding more work becomes a simple process. Bear in mind that leather improves with age and plastic doesn't, and that getting the right size for your work is crucial too; if in doubt, seek advice in the shop. Remember, the portfolio is as important to the freelance illustrator as the limo is to the chauffeur, so this is not the time to economize.

Layout and design

A great portfolio is only as good as the work within it. Buying a fantastically expensive Italian leather folio will be a wasted investment if the work inside is not up to scratch. Making the right decisions on what to include and what to leave out is a tough call for a newcomer and expertise comes with practice and a little trial and error. Seek advice from clients, ask their opinions of your portfolio and adjust accordingly.

If in doubt about a particular piece of work, then you have already answered your own question. Only include work of which you are proud and can talk positively about in a meeting. Don't feel the need to include a project because your mother likes it, only those images that will work hard for you should be included. Put in work that demonstrates your strengths as an illustrator, that shows you can answer a brief and that you have a broad, but individual style or way of working.

Consider putting in work that demonstrates the context in which it was used; don't trim out your image but show the rest of the magazine page, for example. It will give the art director confidence if they can see that you have already been commissioned. Include work that gets you work; some pieces in a portfolio start to shine, watch for those that get the most attention or praise. Think carefully about the order that you place images in, start with a simple but bold and striking piece, perhaps one that people will recognize. Try to end on a similar feel and group images as you progress through the portfolio. Organize according to themes, colour, context or approaches – whatever best suits the work. Lay out images first in a large clear space – on your studio floor if it is clean – so that you can view all of them at once. Make decisions once you have tried a few variations, making lists on paper as you go, so as to remember successful combinations.

It is very easy to include too much work or too little, and creating the right balance comes with experience. A general rule is to include ten to 15 sleeves, giving you room to show 20 to 30 images. Any more than this and some will never be viewed properly, just diluting the experience. Any less than this may leave the viewer wondering if you really can produce the goods.

Consider carefully how you plan and 'design' the layout; for example, a large A3 or B (ledger) portfolio looks best when only one image is used per page. Don't crowd a page; leaving space around an image gives it a chance to 'breathe' and it can be absorbed more easily without the visual distraction of other images. Use the same colour backing-sheet throughout the portfolio; consistency works best in this instance. Resist the temptation to window-mount images, it always looks over-laboured and unnecessary.

Labels can be added to each page, if helpful to the viewer, but ensure that they work well typographically. Keep the type simple and use an uncluttered font such as a sans-serif face like Arial or Helvetica. Range the type to the left and allow for a margin of space around the edge. Place the caption in a standard position on each sleeve, keep the descriptions short and use the same format throughout the portfolio.

5.5
Loose-leaf presentation box portfolio.
Ian Wright
Choosing the best format for a portfolio is paramount. Displaying work in loose sleeves, as is done here, allows each presentation to be tailored to the client.

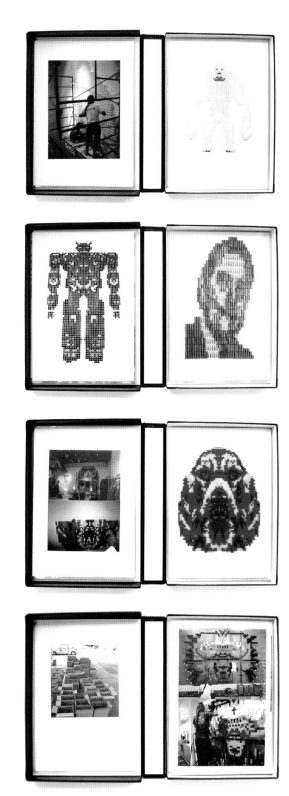

1. The illustrator as artist   2. The medium is the message   3. From outcomes to outlets   4. Communicating ideas   5. Making it happen   6. Production

← Marketing the product and the art of self-promotion   Portfolios   Online presence →

Maintenance and upkeep

Getting a portfolio up and running is only part of the solution, keeping it looking good and performing well is a regular task that needs constant attention. Clean portfolio sleeves with a wipe of lighter fuel on a cotton cloth, replace damaged ones and carefully reposition images that have come unstuck and shifted. All this takes very little time, but can be easily overlooked.

Updating on a regular basis, adding new work and taking out older pieces is necessary to maintain your portfolio's effectiveness. The portfolio may need an entire overhaul as the addition or replacement of just a few images can put the whole running order out of sync. A portfolio really should be this exact.

When preparing a portfolio to be sent out to a client, it is always wise to check that it's in good shape. Fine-tuning the selection to suit the viewer or the potential job that it has been called in for is the next logical step. It is better to have a few more examples of book jackets than CD sleeve designs if the portfolio is going into the art department of a publishing company, for example.

Good practice

Put samples and publicity material in the rear pocket so that art directors and designers have access to a permanent record of your work after a viewing. Make sure that all your contact details are easily visible on the outside of your folio. This is crucial in order to have your book returned by any courier.

For those illustrators that are kept constantly busy with work, setting up an account with a local courier company is a useful asset. Being able to make a call, without any problems, to a company that can be relied upon when an urgent request for a portfolio comes in saves a lot of time and stress.

Portfolio insurance is another worthwhile consideration; not all courier companies are reliable and there are many instances of portfolios going astray within large organizations. Again, although not cheap, insurance should be a consideration for those that have portfolios constantly moving across town or are sending them abroad, something that is occurring more and more often.

Creating duplicates of your portfolio can be incredibly useful if you are in demand. Losing a job because your book can't be sent to the client, as it is sitting in another office somewhere on the other side of town, is very frustrating, but will happen. Creating more than one portfolio is expensive, but a single editorial job will easily pay for it and for the working professional, being ready, prepared and organized must be second nature.

Finally, be a little experimental; add pieces of personal work to the last few sleeves of your portfolio. It is advisable to caption them so that the viewer understands that they are non-commissioned artworks. Showing examples of new ways of working will sit well against the rest of the portfolio of completed and finished projects, and it will demonstrate how your work is creatively developing. If you are present when your portfolio is viewed, be positive and be proud. You need to do your portfolio justice and vice-versa.

> **AUTHOR TIP:**
> **PORTFOLIOS**
>
> — Keep track of exactly where your portfolio is. Label it on the outside with all your contact details.
> — Despatch departments are often responsible for returning your portfolio. Make sure your return info is presented clearly.
> — Stock portfolios with samples to keep for the client. They may only remember your work on the strength of these.
> — A duplicate portfolio prevents loss of earnings when the original is held up elsewhere.
> — Feature your experimental illustrations at the back of your portfolio, and caption them clearly. A good art director will want to see aspects of any shift in approach. It can also be a great talking point.

'…being ready, prepared and organized must be second nature.'

1. The illustrator as artist   2. The medium is the message   3. From outcomes to outlets   4. Communicating ideas   5. Making it happen   6. Production

← Marketing the product and the art of self-promotion   Portfolios   Online presence →

5.6
Leather portfolio.
McFaul
Using a leather, spiral-bound
portfolio allows the running order
of work to be changed easily.

Digital portfolios

Just as important as its physical counterpart, the digital portfolio requires planning, foresight, imagination and an appreciation of the viewer's perspective.

Slide shows

Slide shows are easy to build and use, and are readily available. Search the web for freeware applications that run simple slide-show presentations, or purchase one that does the job, but is inexpensive. Dragging a small digital file onto an open application is as complex as the experience gets. Editing the running order, the time given for each image to appear on screen and simple commands to adjust the transition or dissolve between each image, is likely to be the full extent of any design considerations. This is enough for a professional-looking presentation. Slide shows can be burnt onto CD or emailed.

A key aspect of these types of software applications is that they run independently; they do not require the host computer to have the software pre-installed. This ensures that any machine is capable of viewing the presentation without technical difficulties.

Presentation software

Both Microsoft and Apple also create software packages that can be designed to run with little or no involvement by the viewer. These are ideal for those who choose to create more structured presentations than slide-show software will accommodate. Type can be added, allowing for captions that identify the images, or for titling at the start and end of the show. Contact details can also be created and added, as well as copyright infringement notices.

Good presentation software allows for animation and film to be run directly from the application, allowing for a more accomplished overall look if moving image projects make up an aspect of the portfolio.

These formats also have a second use in the purpose of publicity. The main advantage over printed material is that the initial financial outlay is considerably less. Allowing for constant change and updating, these formats enable ease of creation for a specific audience or client and can potentially showcase many more images than a traditional leather-bound book.

The combined price of a CD, an envelope and the postage stamps is far less than a courier bill for the same journey and financial demands do not dictate that the CD is returned. This is a workable portfolio that acts well as a publicity and marketing tool as well.

**AUTHOR TIP:
DIGITAL PORTFOLIOS**

- Create any digital presentation in up-to-the-minute software applications that can be read by both PC and Macintosh platforms.
- Test your presentation on various computers and screens to view as your client will see it – do this before you start making copies.
- Ask your regular clients if they respond to this type of presentation – new media companies and animation and production houses will be quite used to viewing work in this format – book publishers will not be.
- Make the experience of viewing your digital portfolio a user-friendly one. Potential clients will not hang around waiting for your presentation to start, nor will they continue if the navigation is complex or unusable.

Online presence

A website is a must. Increasingly, so are blogs and social-media profiles. Getting these things working in a useful and meaningful way takes vision and an understanding of the medium.

Before you even start to consider your own online presence, research plenty of other illustrators' profiles. Start by getting URLs from illustration organizations; the Association of Illustrators in London has links to its members' sites. Gather more links from details published in annuals and Google-search for direct access to sites. Learn from how others use the web as a medium for housing a portfolio before creating your own.

When building a website, establish who is going to design it; if you are doing it yourself, make sure that you set yourself realistic goals and a timeframe to produce the work in. Investigate employing a web designer, they will have far more experience and bring expertise to the project – perhaps a recent graduate just entering the profession and looking to broaden his or her own portfolio. Friends that are designers may be interested in trading illustrations for website work, so be up front and ask.

Content

Consider the content of your profiles before working on their look and feel. Think carefully about the job that you would like your sites to accomplish. If purely a portfolio site, it may just contain images and captions but this could be a missed opportunity.

Other content to include might be a short welcome introduction and then a brief biography, including some information about your education, recent projects, upcoming exhibitions, etc. Work out how to group your work into sections; all editorial commissions could be in one area, book covers and design company projects in another. Having an area that is used to showcase new and uncommissioned work can be instrumental in allowing others to see the direction that your new work is taking.

Easy access to your contact details is important, although it is safest to only publish email contact info – remember you are unable to control exactly who can view your site. Another useful area of content is a page containing links to other websites that you recommend. Links from your site to others may mean that they also provide links back to your site, thus increasing the amount of potential traffic. It is advisable to make contact before creating a link, this will ensure that a link back is considered, too.

Some illustrators find that the extra-curricular work of creating limited-edition digital or screen-prints, or even a small range of T-shirts can be successfully marketed on a website and start to form the basis for a small online shop. It is unlikely that business demands will ever overflow into a major commitment, but there may be enough interest to warrant time and finances being directed towards a shop as part of the overall presence being created.

Design, navigation and layout

The best advice for those working on their first website is to keep things simple. Nothing is more disconcerting or off-putting than a badly designed website that is difficult to navigate. Map out a simple diagram of the basic structure before work on the site begins. Identify each of the separate areas as a box and link each box with lines to show how the viewer will navigate the site. It may well take numerous attempts to complete the diagram, but the exercise will ensure that questions regarding content and structure are raised, if not truly answered, at this stage.

The overall design of the site needs addressing soon after the structure diagram has been resolved. Knowing how the site will look and feel early on will be an advantage, resolving design considerations is easiest early on in a project. The design should complement the illustration work it houses and not distract the viewer from the work. Keep text to a minimum, as most people don't enjoy scrolling through pages and pages of copy on-screen. Create captions to identify the work's key points and ensure all images sit comfortably on screen without any need for scrolling.

1. The illustrator as artist   2. The medium is the message   3. From outcomes to outlets   4. Communicating ideas   5. Making it happen   6. Production

← Portfolios   Online presence   Avenues for self-promotion →

Navigation should be easy to use without being too childishly obvious. Ensure that all areas of the site can be reached without the need for the viewer to use the 'back' button of the Web browser. Think about the route that viewers will take when accessing all aspects of your site and make sure that no area takes more than a few clicks of the mouse to get to. People want to access information quickly with the minimum of fuss.

Although most users will have fast connections to the Internet, some will not and this needs to be taken into account when considering content. Make sure that pages download quickly by keeping the file sizes for images small and don't add unnecessary animated details.

Maintenance, upkeep and promotion

Just as a real-world portfolio needs constant attention, so does an online version. Keeping your profiles up to date with new work and forthcoming exhibitions and events is crucial and should not be too time consuming. Checking that sites view well on a range of different machines, screens and different browsers is part of the development process, but should be done periodically once the site is up and running as well.

An online profile that is not promoted effectively is about as useful as having no profile at all. Promotion can be as simple as ensuring that keywords are embedded in the front page; this is where search engines look for information about a site and identify what it contains. Using a range of keywords will help broaden the appeal to search engines, but be realistic; the word 'illustrator' reveals over three million results in Google, whereas 'editorial illustrator, New York,' limits the search to 100,000.

5.7
Website for Trina Dalziel.
This personal and visually
dynamic website clearly shows
the style of the illustrator. It
is both interactive and easy to
navigate. There are clear sections
to demonstrate the breadth of
the work that the illustrator
undertakes.

Promoting your website with a postcard may seem like a backwards step technologically, but can really increase awareness and traffic. Emailing a link to your site and including some low-res images will increase awareness too. Without an audience a website will just sit on the hard shoulder of the information superhighway without any place to go.

Both analogue and digital portfolios are the lifeblood of the working illustrator, without them working hard on your behalf, it can be impossible to win even the first commission.

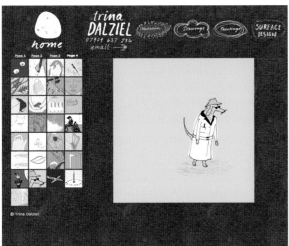

1. The illustrator as artist   2. The medium is the message   3. From outcomes to outlets   4. Communicating ideas   5. Making it happen   6. Production

← Portfolios   Online presence   Avenues for self-promotion →

5.7

Avenues for self-promotion

The self-promoting illustrator should plan to make an impact that leads to a request to view a portfolio of work, (with or without the illustrator present), a decision to click on a website for more illustration samples, or even to directly commission work. Publicity is never created with the intention of securing a job for life or to set out an in-depth professional history or profile, so simplicity is the key. It is never wise to send a long resume or CV: it should be the quality of the work that dictates the approach. Many art school graduates are pleased to announce where they studied and what degree they got, and are frustrated when they realize that it is purely the quality of the portfolio of work that interests the viewer.

Creating an annual desktop or wall-mounted calendar, for example, can work as an effective promotional device; they are useful objects as well as a daily reminder of the illustrator's work. Remember though, that every print company, photographic agency, stock-image library and facilities house will have the same idea and probably bigger budgets, so that on the first Monday of January every art director in town will spend most of the morning opening large, well-sealed envelopes with calendars inside.

Pop-up or stand-up promo pieces that are intended to attract attention as desktop novelties invariably don't stand the test of time. Objects that require construction will probably remain unbuilt. Creating a device that works well, that inspires, surprises or raises a smile will, however, produce results. Clients like to be impressed, are flattered and will appreciate the time and energy involved in creating a promotional item that communicates effectively. Illustrators that create posters, boxes of images, concertina hand-made books and any number of elaborate promo objects inevitably receive requests to visit with a portfolio of work. The secret is in creating a promotional object that is well targeted, well designed and well worth receiving.

5.8
Contact, Contact Publishing. To guarantee entry into an annual, opt for the pay-and-display option – normally published within the first quarter of a new calendar year and mailed directly to all top industry companies on your behalf.

1. The illustrator as artist 2. The medium is the message 3. From outcomes to outlets 4. Communicating ideas **5. Making it happen** 6. Production

← Online presence Avenues for self-promotion Illustration agency representation →

The annuals

Annuals offer another distinct area of investigation in the search for self-promotional nirvana. There are three different types of annual that illustrators can aspire to have their work included in and all do the job, albeit in slightly different ways.

The first, and definitely the most aspirational of the three, is the annual of work that has been selected and judged by distinguished industry peers. These annuals are compiled and published by organizations like the Society of Illustrators in New York and the Association of Illustrators in London, and are normally launched at an exhibition of work from the book. The SOI in New York was founded in 1901 and has published over 47 annuals, simply entitled *Illustrators*, whilst the AOI in London, formed in 1973, has published 28 editions of its annual, *Images*.

There is stiff competition in every category for entry to the SOI and AOI annuals each year. For many, the call for entries has become something of an annual ritual, despite never knowing what may catch the judges' eyes to make it into the final selection, and there is never a shortage of those hoping to make it into the book and accompanying exhibition.

The second category of annual also works as a full-colour index of illustrators' work and contact details, but there is a fee for entry. These are normally determined by a page rate, and it is this fact that identifies the annual as being more representative of the entire industry rather than the best of the work being produced. These annuals show work to suit all tastes, but not all of it will be very good.

The third type of annual is more restrictive as entry is entirely reserved for illustration agents to book pages in. This has benefits for those that use the annual; they know that each and every illustrator featured can be contacted through their agents. Many clients like to deal only through an agency, but more on that issue later in this chapter.

Annuals can be expensive to enter, only appear once a year and can give the impression of a creative cattle market, but they do have one major benefit that outweighs any negative perceptions. Annuals are distributed free of charge to those in the industry who commission illustration; they are sent to advertising agencies, book publishers and design companies, and are always kept and referred to. Targeting and reaching an audience this broad in one hit with a professional piece of promotion is never easy, and for this reason alone inclusion in an annual is a must.

Another reason to consider the annual is their run-ons. A run-on is exactly what it sounds like; exact copies of individual pages of the book printed as extra, one-sided sheets. As a useful incentive for inclusion, the publishers of the annuals build supplying 500–1000 run-ons of the artist's page into the overall cost. This means that the individual illustrator then has a ready-made piece of publicity for marketing purposes.

Illustration agency representation

If the whole idea of maintaining a strong marketing and publicity campaign, keeping mailing lists up-to-date, and coordinating the delivery as well as the upkeep of your portfolios seems unmanageable, then it may be wise to consider approaching an illustration agency for representation.

Agencies are a useful link to the professional world for those illustrators that are either too busy to spend time undertaking the business side of the discipline, find that they are just not very good at it or do not enjoy meeting new clients on a regular basis. Having an external 'face' is an exceptionally useful tool for many illustrators, so that for this, and other contributing factors, artists are prepared to shed a percentage of their fee for the service.

The positive aspects

Debates about the relative pros and cons of agency representation continue to surface, but for those happily housed within an agency portfolio, most of the issues are positive. Being able to hand over the financial negotiations of a project to someone often far more adept and practiced can be a real relief for some. Having an agent involved in quoting a fee for a potential or real project can increase the final fee; many illustrators have issues understanding the marketplace and exactly what their work is worth. It is not uncommon for an agency to command and receive fees over and above the illustrator's own perception of what the fee should be. This can mean that agency representation can pay for itself; an agent who can charge 25 per cent higher fees than a solo artist is, indirectly, creating their own percentage from a project.

Good agents relate to their client base, they know their market and fully understand the business of illustration. The best agents have spent time building relationships with art directors, art buyers and designers and are usually on friendly terms with them. Clients trust good agents, and will seek advice about the most appropriate artist for a particular project. The agent can be the first person called when a commission is forthcoming. Some agents have been in the business for many years and have established themselves as experts in the field – this is not easy to replicate as a solo artist.

Most agencies share the burden and cost of publicity with their artists, a rule-of-thumb being that an agency pays the same percentage towards the costs as the percentage that they take in fees. Some will pay for one major agency publicity publication each year in addition, but each company has its own take on what they offer. Many artists, when the relationship works well, find that most work starts to come through the agency and so feel less of a need for their own self-promotional material. This, in itself, can be a huge release.

Agencies deliver portfolios and quote on potential projects. Both tasks can be time consuming and will not generate income unless developing into real commissions. Illustrators running their own business affairs can waste much time chasing jobs that don't happen. The artist often overlooks this aspect of agency representation, but it is this job that is the foundation of an agency's success and reputation.

ADVANTAGES OF AGENCY REPRESENTATION

— Agents are unafraid to demand the best possible fees. They don't get embarrassed – the higher the fee the bigger their percentage.
— Although agents can command between 20–30 per cent of the final fee as their own, they are likely to gain a higher fee than a lone illustrator could.
— Some advertising agents will only deal with an artist through their agent – no agent can mean no work for some companies.
— Agents have experience of managing careers – they can advise you what direction to consider taking your work in. They see many more portfolios than you ever can.
— Many illustrators hate having to attend meetings – they don't enjoy the process and agents willingly take on this burden of responsibility.

Agency representation also means the artist avoids the task of chasing up purchase orders and paperwork related to a project. Producing detailed invoices with information about the parameters of the usage of a particular artwork can be no fun either. Constantly phoning accounts departments after 30 days to enquire why an invoice remains unpaid is a weary and soul-destroying task and an efficient agent takes care of all of this.

The negative aspects

Not all aspects of agency representation appeal to every artist. Illustration agencies are businesses, and in order to stay in business they must represent artists that are in fashion and will win commissions. Agencies are less likely to take creative risks when considering new artists and this can have the effect of stifling the industry by ignoring emerging talent.

Agents will expect artists interested in joining them to already have a substantial back catalogue and a regular supply of new work. Even with this, they may demand that an artist works solely through the agency and hand over all client details at the start of the arrangement. Another real drawback can be that not all clients are prepared to work with agents – some have a reputation for being hard-nosed and demanding unreasonable fees – and will only work directly with artists.

Issues of communication are another drawback, as many prefer to keep the lines of communication as short as possible. An agent may be seen as another link in a chain that can so easily lead to game of Chinese Whispers.

Whatever the ups and downs of agents and the roles that they play, it is wise to get first-hand knowledge and experience. If looking for an agent, aim to meet with as many as possible, send in samples to agencies that best suit your own approach and methods of work. Seek advice from illustrators that are represented, look at the range and depth of the illustrators already with agencies that interest you. Be prepared and be knowledgeable. If you are talented, it is likely that more than one agency will be interested in representing you; don't go with the first offer, consider them all and then decide.

DISADVANTAGES OF AGENCY REPRESENTATION

— Some clients refuse to work through agencies – they want direct contact with the illustrator they wish to work with, believing that the best work is produced with a shorter chain of communication.
— There are clients that begrudge paying the higher fees that an agent may command – they see agents as mercenaries!
— The financial pressure to maintain high-profile marketing can be too great, as well as being creatively limiting for some illustrators. Many prefer to set their own personal direction for marketing and publicity.
— Some agents demand that all work goes through the agency – meaning that a percentage of the fees from regular work from contracts and clients built up over time is liable to be paid to the agent.
— Not all illustrators trust agents – having a businessman tackle issues of creativity whilst acting as a middleman just seems inappropriate to some.

1. The illustrator as artist 2. The medium is the message 3. From outcomes to outlets 4. Communicating ideas 5. Making it happen 6. Production

← Avenues for self-promotion Illustration agency representation Presentation techniques →

5.9

Presentation techniques

Whether with an agent or working solo, you will have to spend time making many presentations to clients on a regular basis, starting from the point of that very first meeting.

Presentation techniques are no mystery, but can prove problematic for some artists. Despite an art school training that can require constant justification of a piece of work, often in group situations, many illustrators do not communicate clearly in meetings with their own clients.

It is important to be confident about your work when presenting your portfolio, although there is a fine line between confidence and arrogance; show self-belief and be positive about what you do and how you work. A friendly manner is much more appealing than a cool stand-offish nature, as many clients choose whom to work with based on personality as much as portfolio work.

Speak slowly and clearly, and aim to inform during a review of your portfolio or when you present visuals or final artwork to a client. It is wise to remember a few short background stories behind one or two pieces of work. Clients may view your work and meet with you in a busy studio, if a meeting room is unavailable. Don't let this phase you. You may be interrupted by others in the studio asking questions or phones ringing. Try to take it all in your stride and be professional; sulking or storming out will get you nowhere.

Demonstrate enthusiasm for your client's business as well as your own, and research the company that you are meeting with; look at recent projects, ask questions and make comments that show you are knowledgeable about their work and current issues too. At the same time, be aware of the need to listen, as when nervous it is easy to talk too much. If you find yourself in this situation, try to slow down and take stock.

Don't be afraid to take notes, as it is useful to have something on paper to refer to after the meeting. With the possibility of so much information being relayed in a relatively short space of time, it is very easy to forget key aspects. Take a notepad and pen and start the meeting with them to hand.

Do ensure that you look professional: the design and advertising worlds are fairly relaxed and informal environments, but it is important to look and feel appropriately dressed. Personal hygiene should be not be an issue for discussion, being clean and tidy must be a given. Some meetings will require a business suit; a presentation of final artwork to the end client of a project is a case in point. Just like the extra duplicate portfolio that sits in the studio, having a change of clothes ready, in case of an urgent meeting can be a blessing.

Overall, it is important to be yourself, but a confident, approachable and motivated version. Switch it on when you enter a meeting, if need be; it can and will make a difference.

5.9
Images of Lichfield.
Callum Ives
When making a presentation to a client, some illustrators prefer to finish a series of illustrations. These can then be shown to the person commissioning the work for them to choose from.

Case study: Ben Kelly

Ben Kelly is a professional illustrator, artist and educator. His work has featured in newspapers, magazines and greeting cards; he also exhibits his paintings in galleries across the UK.

The commission

Ben was commissioned as artist in residence at Manchester City Football Club. His brief was to document the match day experiences of Manchester City supporters.

The approach

In response to the brief, Ben produced initial sketchbook work at the football ground. He also used photography, where appropriate, and used this visual information to form the basis for the composite paintings he completed later.

Approval

Throughout the residency, Ben showed his work in progress to the club.

Conclusion

The paintings that Ben created during his residency at Manchester City Football Club were exhibited at the National Football Museum and The City of Manchester Museum at the football ground.

5.10
'Painting the blues'. Sketchbook roughs and final painting.
Ben Kelly
Ben Kelly's paintings capture the atmosphere and excitement of a Manchester City football match.

5.10

1. The illustrator as artist   2. The medium is the message   3. From outcomes to outlets   4. Communicating ideas   5. Making it happen   6. Production

← Presentation techniques   Case study: Ben Kelly   Try it yourself... →

Try it yourself…

Making it happen

Self-promotion and presentation are skills that are developed over time and continually updated. This exercise will help you to consider who you are and how best to promote yourself.

Materials

Photographs of yourself, paper, illustration materials (pens, paints, etc), camera. Long sheet of paper folded into a concertina.

The brief: Self-promotion concertina

Who are you? Start by creating a number of thumbnails/ rough sketches of things that relate to you. These could be your favourite foods, colours, sounds, seasons, drinks, flower, shoes, mood – the list is endless.

Once you have developed lots of small images, make a concertina booklet to use as your promotional vehicle. This can be as small as you wish but should not exceed A5 or Legal size when folded. You may wish to create a different image on every page or one long linear image – but it must be about you.

Questions in summary

1. How can an illustrator promote their own work?
2. What are the advantages of self-promotion?
3. How do your favourite illustrators promote their work?
4. How would you like people to find out about your work?

1. The illustrator as artist   2. The medium is the message   3. From outcomes to outlets   4. Communicating ideas   5. Making it happen   6. Production

← Try it yourself…   Questions in summary

Chapter 6 — Production

Illustrators can be technophobes; they can immerse themselves in artistic creation, but shut themselves away from the realities and formalities of production and technology issues. However, gaining a broad foundation of knowledge gives the illustrator an awareness that brings freedom, flexibility and the understanding required to meet the technical challenges of life in the profession.

Essential kit

As previously discussed, illustrators work in a variety and combination of different media, and most start to find the materials that they feel an affinity with during the latter part of their art and design education. A growing understanding of how materials behave is part of that journey, but one aspect missing in the education programmes of many design institutions is an in-depth teaching of production issues. In order to discuss these demands, it is important to start with the basic components and materials that illustrators use daily in the studio.

Basics

Find the materials that work for you. Try a range of products and brands, but be clear which ones give you the results that you are happy with. There is no top brand of acrylic paint, no definitive make of pencil; there are only the materials that you work best with. Whether working with spray paint and finding that a particular nozzle works in the most satisfying way, or discovering that a certain squeegee drags the ink in a more effective manner, it is about choice.

Trial and error are crucial to discovering the right tools and materials. Learn to follow your instinct and don't be afraid to ask the opinions of others. Be prepared to give some materials the benefit of the doubt as not many can be mastered in minutes and most need time to adjust your working methods to them. When you find a specific brush or shade of paint that works, it can be a heart-warming moment. The same feeling presents itself when an aspect of a software application is mastered, and you perform a task that moves a piece of work forward in a new direction.

It is rare to find a shop that sells all the right products under one roof and it can take visits to various shops to find the particular type, brand or range that you require. There is something about the atmosphere of a good art supply shop that evokes feelings of excitement and awe, like a child in a sweet shop. Shopping online is time-saving and convenient, but can be a sterile experience in comparison. Wandering the aisles of Pearl Paint off Canal Street in New York, the London Graphic Centre in Covent Garden or Tokyu Hands in the Shinjuku district of Tokyo is an experience that can't be replicated on-screen.

There are some items of kit that have simply been essential must-haves for the illustrator since the discipline's birth. There are others that have become essential in recent years with the advent and introduction of digital working methods.

Analogue essentials

Even for the digital artist, paper is normally the starting point. Paper comes in a multitude of formats, weights and finishes and the choice of stock is dependent on the usage. There is little point in attempting to use watercolour paints in a bleed-proof marker pad, common sense is the overruling factor most of the time.

All artists understand, or rapidly find out, the difference between a hard and soft lead pencil, how to fix a charcoal drawing on location or the benefits of a putty rubber over an office eraser; the trick is in adapting the materials to suit the user.

1. The illustrator as artist   2. The medium is the message   3. From outcomes to outlets   4. Communicating ideas   5. Making it happen   **6. Production**

Essential kit Studio set-up →

Digital essentials

It is now impossible to consider an illustrator successfully working without access to digital tools, an idea unthinkable even at the end of the twentieth century. Whether an artist creates all work on-screen or scans in original drawings to be reworked or coloured in the computer, or they simply attach final artworks into emails to deliver to the client, almost every aspect of the process can be digitized.

When considering the purchase of digital equipment it pays, yet again, to seek advice. Most people tend to buy what they need as and when they require it, updating and upgrading as they go. Most students will have used equipment made available during their studies and will find, on graduating, that they have to purchase some kit for the first time.

Speaking to other illustrators and getting recommendations pays dividends. There is very little point in buying a top spec, high-end computer that is capable of rendering 3D graphics in seconds, at a huge cost if you work in watercolour and only intend to use the machine to send artwork via email and conduct Web-based research.

The computer

Basic digital requirements will always include a computer and the biggest decisions will start with making the choice between buying a PC or Apple Mac and choosing between desktop or laptop. Personal preference will dictate which route is taken, but considering a portable machine is worthwhile. Being able to work at the studio and in the home, as well as working and making presentations on the move, is a major bonus. Laptop computers can be locked away overnight to avoid theft and can be plugged into large desktop monitors when a larger working area is needed. They may have less raw power than a desktop model, but for most illustrators they are more than adequate.

The scanner

A scanner – to input hand-drawn images and found printed reference into the computer – is essential, although a small A4 or Letter version is all that is normally needed. For those who aim to draw directly into a software application, a drawing tablet is essential kit. They can take a little time to fully master, but many experienced digital illustrators swear by them.

The printer

Outputting images on a digital printer is important when keeping a portfolio up to date, but far less important as a tool for checking colours. The process that a budget digital printer goes through in creating colours for print is very different from the four-colour printing process used in the industrial off-set lithography used by publishers.

The camera

A good digital camera is a must, both as a useful tool for inputting images, and for shooting reference material. Being able to capture the figure in various poses to then bring into an application for drawing or retouching makes figure work much less time-consuming and less dependent on traditional skills. A recent upsurge in vector-drawn and traced figures in illustrations has been directly brought about by the relative simplicity of this process.

Backing up

Backing up, storing and archiving work is a boring, but necessary aspect of digital work. It can take some freelancers a major computer crash and loss of files before they are ready to begin a routine of regular back-ups. Although wise to copy work files on to an external hard drive, these are not indestructible and must not be regarded as completely error-free places to archive work. A small drive that fits in a bag or pocket is better value per megabyte than a small keyring USB storage device, but it is also vital to back up onto CD or DVD and create duplicate copies of each disc too. Get into the habit of keeping one set of data in an alternative location; it is best to be thorough before a worst-case scenario occurs.

1. The illustrator as artist   2. The medium is the message   3. From outcomes to outlets   4. Communicating ideas   5. Making it happen   **6. Production**

Essential kit Studio set-up →

Studio set-up

Solo or group?

There is an important decision that every illustrator must make; it can be dictated by working methods, by financial considerations or by personal choice and it is about the location of the studio. For some the studio will be, at its simplest, the kitchen table or the back bedroom, while for others it may be a rented desk space within a design company, or a shared loft-style studio in a cool part of town. Finding the place that best suits your needs is fundamental to creating an environment conducive to creative working. Setting up a studio can be challenging and exciting, but planning ahead is crucial.

Freelance illustration is a predominantly solo discipline; much of the work is undertaken in a space away from the client and delivered at the end of the process. Until email became the normal mode of delivery, illustrators tended to migrate towards the cities where most commissions were likely to be forthcoming. If they chose not to and lived and worked in another part of the country, they adjusted their working methods to allow for delivery times. Although email has made delivery instant and the mobile phone has ensured that communication can be a constant, many illustrators still prefer to work in urban areas. This may be related to the need or desire to meet face-to-face with the art director or designer on a project, or it may go back to issues of self-promotion and the ease in getting to and from presentations laden with a portfolio.

Deciding on a solo or group studio is determined by choice. Many illustrators demand the solace and silence of a space that is uninterrupted by fellow artists, whilst others find it impossible to concentrate without the buzz and noise of a shared space. It is wise not to rush into the excitement of creating a group studio without having had some experience of working in one. Equally, spending time and money converting a spare bedroom into a studio, if completely unused to working alone, can be a commitment and undertaking that proves to be unnecessary.

There are benefits and drawbacks to both types of studio set-up and both need some careful consideration. Working alongside others can provide an environment that is inspiring, interesting and supportive. It can also be off-putting and disturbing as well as frustrating. For those that choose to work alone, the benefits of the solo studio may be in the freedom and personal space that the situation allows. Drawbacks, however, include having no face-to-face, one-to-one conversations or feedback about an idea or work-in-progress from a sympathetic ear. Hours may pass without direct communication with another individual, although for many, this situation may be a positive asset.

For those who choose to join or set up a group studio, having costs of shared equipment and facilities can be financially beneficial and can lead to greater access to technology that may be out of reach for the solo trader. Buying one very good digital camera, renting a photocopier, installing a mini-kitchen or investing in a table tennis table are far simpler spread across a group.

Communication tools

Whether going it alone or joining a group there are some essentials that require immediate attention. Having a mobile phone, with credit, is a must, as is a studio phone that can divert to the mobile. Increasingly, mobiles have email technology built into them and this can be a real plus when out at appointments for an entire day; some clients' first choice for communication is email.

A fast Internet link is not to be overlooked – sending artwork via email, especially large files, can take valuable time. Occasionally company firewalls bounce emails back if they don't recognize the sender or the file size is too large. Managing these issues without a wide bandwidth can take crucial time when delivering work.

The work space

Work spaces vary but an illustrator's studio is rarely a dull place. Digital technology appeared to turn creative design studios into sterile office environments with huge casings of grey and cream plastic, housing humming computer kit and monitors. The illustrator's studio, in contrast, appears to have retained much of the fun and frivolity of the art school. It is a fact that design groups have to entertain their clients, who may be deeply concerned to enter a less-than-professional environment, whereas illustrators create spaces they feel comfortable working in. Without the pressure of visiting clients, the studio becomes an extension of creative expression for the illustrator. It is not uncommon to see wild collections of stuffed animals, toys and model kits, thrift-store ceramics, comic art posters, rubber stamp kits and the like adorning the walls and shelves of the studio.

Illustrators can be messy; paints, inks, scraps of tracing paper, masking tape, glues, coloured crayons and sticky-backed paper are likely to be strewn across many surfaces. It is in amongst this variety of old-school materials that the computer and related peripherals sit.

Safety issues

Setting up a work space that performs properly, that allows for creativity, experimentation and the everyday work tasks of creating illustrations needs to be done with a number of factors in mind. A dedicated space for thinking, researching and the tasks of invoicing and payment chasing, as well as portfolio organization, must be part of the equation. Health and safety considerations such as correct height of monitor and keyboard position to ensure unharmful posture, are as important as ensuring safe working practices are adopted for the handling of potentially hazardous materials, such as spray paints and adhesives. Positioning a monitor away from direct light and making sure that electrical cables are not trailing across a floor are all requirements of a safe working space.

1. The illustrator as artist 2. The medium is the message 3. From outcomes to outlets 4. Communicating ideas 5. Making it happen 6. Production

← Essential kit Studio set-up Resources and references →

Resources and references

Illustrators need inspiration and reference material. The notion that artists pick ideas and themes out of thin air and then create visuals without referring to real or photographed imagery is one held by some clients, but the reality is somewhat different.

Every illustrator builds his or her own reference library, whether trawling second-hand bookstores for out-of-print examples of 1970s car manuals, or out shooting and collecting photographic reference of street signage, an illustrator constantly adds to the library of images and ephemera. Old DIY magazines, instructional leaflets, stamp collections, record sleeves, matchbox labels; they are all collected and referenced.

Housing collections and libraries is never easy, as illustrators tend to require organized space to store and display objects and files; a particular colour combination or layout may be called upon at any time for inspiration. Some illustrators use storage boxes, some create large archive files for printed ephemera to be contained in, but whichever type of device or system is utilized, it plays a vital part in the process of creating illustrations.

With hard drives increasing in capacity on an annual basis, storing digital photographic reference is becoming easier and many are turning to this method of organizing their research. Many illustrators, however, would argue that there is no substitute for the real object. Feeling the quality of the paper, breathing in the scent of that print and handling a real object are part of the process of inspiration.

Referencing a particular image has never been quicker or simpler – huge royalty-free files of photographic reference and imagery are available on collections of CDs. The same is true for clip art and Victorian engravings and most are available from book stores, computer warehouses, traditional art and design suppliers, as well as the Internet. Searching for visual reference online takes seconds with Google image search, one of the most important research tools to emerge for the illustrator in the last decade.

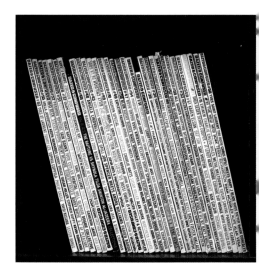

1. The illustrator as artist   2. The medium is the message   3. From outcomes to outlets   4. Communicating ideas   5. Making it happen   **6. Production**

← Studio set-up   Resources and references   Production tips →

Production tips

There are enough potential production tips to warrant filling an entire book, and shelves groan under the weight of titles offering readers purported shortcuts to learning and then mastering software. There are also numerous magazines on monthly sale offering software tricks and tips to readers, but many of the most frequent lessons and some of the best advice are often not highlighted or tailored specifically for illustrators. There is very little substitute for learning on the job and valuable experience gained throughout initial projects can be put to greater use as commissions appear more regularly.

Working in the field of illustration requires some specialist knowledge and for the beginner it can feel like a minefield. The best advice is to learn some technical terms and the terminology used in print and production, and understand what they all mean. If you are not sure what 'bleed' (when an image is printed to the edge of the paper) is, for example, don't be afraid to ask. It is common to meet designers and art directors that use production terms and phrases so regularly that they can forget that newcomers may not yet fully grasp the language. Never leave a briefing, however, without a full understanding of the technical expectations; mistakes can be time-consuming and costly, so ensure that communication is clear or fully explained and if it is not, ask.

Colour management

Start as you mean to go on and ensure that files are set up correctly before you commence a project, it is far better to do this before getting in too deep. A common mistake is to ignore the file formats required for the production of the artwork at the design stage. Setting up files for print in CMYK breaks colours into percentages that can be achieved from the four-colour set of cyan (C), magenta (M), yellow (Y) and black (K), and this is how most colour jobs are printed.

Special colours

On some occasions fifth and sixth colours are added to the print process. These are known as 'specials' and have to be specified correctly from Pantone reference charts. Special colours are used when it is impossible to create a colour from the four-colour set, such as metallics or fluorescents, or when it is vital to match an existing colour that needs to appear in its purest form. Specified special colours are mixed by hand and applied on a separate plate from the four plates made for CMYK. Specials are only likely to be used for specialist projects; it is not possible to specify silver ink for an illustration to accompany a magazine article, for example. It may be appropriate, though, to discuss the possibility for an image of a magazine cover, but this discussion should take place with the art director at the briefing stage and not just presented as a secondary thought with the final artwork. Adding special colours always adds to the print and production costs.

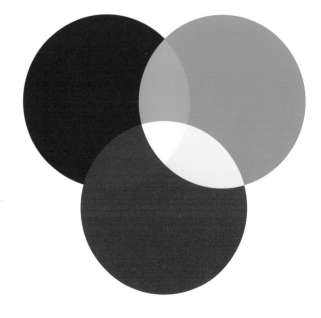

6.1
Additive primaries.
When light is emitted (such as from a screen), colour is created by the three primaries, red, green and blue. When these three colours mix, they create white light.

Screen-based work

[F]or work that will not be printed, but shown on-screen [o]nly (websites, TV or animation, for example), files will [n]eed to be set up in the RGB format. Here, all colours are [c]reated from properties and combinations of red (R), green [(G)] and blue (B). Red, green and blue are the primary [c]olours of light and are referred to as primary colours [o]r as the additive primaries. Although the RGB format [w]orks for screen-based illustration projects, it is wise not [t]o trust the representation of colours on your monitor [u]nless it has been well calibrated. Once calibrated, a good [m]onitor will reproduce colours for screen accurately but [w]ill always present an approximation of any project that [w]ill be going to print. It is therefore important to check [t]he percentage breakdown of each colour used against a [P]antone print swatch guide or against printed examples [f]rom previous projects.

File formats

File formats are important to get right; ensure that you only give the client flattened images without access to the individual layers that make up the project. This gives the illustrator some protection against misuse by a client and it is best not to provide temptation. Ensuring changes or alterations required are made by the illustrator alone is the goal and files that allow clients freedom to scale and print, but not open and alter are the safest option. The illustrator retains copyright on every image they create, unless otherwise stated, and not allowing others to alter or change an image offers some protection against illustrations appearing in print that devalue the work of the illustrator.

The final file format is dependent on the type of project – some clients prefer artwork to arrive as a TIFF (Tagged Image File Format), others request JPEGs (Joint Photographic Experts Group), or EPS (Encapsulated PostScript) files; the only true course of action is to check before embarking on the project. Ensure that the resolution is correct too; creating a piece of work in 72 dpi when it is expected in 300 dpi is a common, but easily avoidable, mistake. Most production issues can be resolved through tight communication; lapses in communication can often result in unexpected, unwanted and unbelievable results.

1. The illustrator as artist   2. The medium is the message   3. From outcomes to outlets   4. Communicating ideas   5. Making it happen   **6. Production**

← Resources and references   Production tips   Legal tips →

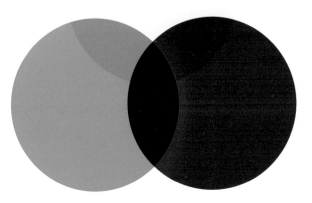

6.2
Subtractive primaries
When light is reflected (such as from a printed surface), colour is created by the three primaries, cyan, magenta and yellow. When these three colours mix, they create black.

Legal tips

An often overlooked aspect of the day-to-day running and long-term organization of a career in illustration is in the legalities and liabilities surrounding tax issues. Despite illustration rarely falling into a list of careers that have difficulties in keeping the right side of the law, it is wise to know and fully understand all potential implications associated with the legalities.

If you plan to work in illustration, then it is vital to ensure that your local tax office knows that you are trading for business. There is an unwritten rule that states that creative people have problems with numbers, figures and maths – get yourself organized early and ensure that you set your business up correctly from the start.

Firstly find your local tax office and turn to them for advice about exactly how you should set up your business – make sure that everything is taken into account. Normally you'll not be expected to pay any tax until your annual turnover reaches a certain level – this can be hit quite soon if you get busy, so be prepared.

Enlist the services of an accountant – take advice and recommendations from other illustrators. Use someone who has some understanding of the profession and the possible implications for your tax issues. A good accountant will recommend particular courses of action, explaining pitfalls before they arise and pointing out methods of eliminating unnecessary tax burdens. They may command a hefty fee for their services, but that expense should be paid for out of the savings they make you.

An accountant will advise you of exactly what details your invoices should cover – obvious details include your name and address. Less obvious details, but as important is that the invoice carries an invoice number – a legal requirement. An accountant can also advise you of terms and conditions that you may wish to apply to your clients, although further expertise can also be sought from a solicitor.

Access to a good solicitor will come in handy should you need information and advice regarding copyright issues – ensuring that you retain copyright over your images is a fundamental right. Working out exactly what to charge for usage or for full copyright of an image can be tricky – an agent can come in handy here or at least advice from a solicitor with links to a professional industry body such as the Association of Illustrators, or the Society of Illustrators.

Ignorance is no defence – make sure that you fully understand just how to set your business up legally. Being aware of what to do and not do is vital – be prepared.

6.3
'Spires'
Amy Jones
It is important to be aware of all the financial and legal pitfalls before embarking on life as an illustrator.

1. The illustrator as artist   2. The medium is the message   3. From outcomes to outlets   4. Communicating ideas   5. Making it happen   6. Production

← Production tips Legal tips Case study: Howard Read →

6.3

Case study: Howard Read

Howard Read is a professional illustrator and educator. His editorial work has featured in *The Financial Times*, *The Independent*, *The Sunday Times* and *The Economist*.

The commission

Howard was emailed by the art director of *The Guardian Weekend* magazine on a Wednesday afternoon and aske if he would like to illustrate an article in the 'How to…' column, entitled 'How to… Decorate'. The article intende to take a humorous look at how humans and animals decorate themselves and their environment. Before confirming, Howard discussed all aspects of the commission, including rough work, final artwork, size of the work, fee and copy. A deadline for two days later was given.

6.4
Editorial illustration for
The Guardian Weekend magazine.
Howard Read
If an illustrator can complete a
commission in time and within
budget, they are more likely to be
approached again in the future.

1. The illustrator as artist 2. The medium is the message 3. From outcomes to outlets 4. Communicating ideas 5. Making it happen **6. Production**

← Legal tips   Case study: Howard Read   Try it yourself... →

Initial response

Howard started by reading the copy carefully and making notes on ideas and possible elements to feature within the illustration. He started drawing initial responses, including potential figures and other elements. The ideas were then drawn in black and white as a rough compositional layout and sent to the art director at *The Guardian* for approval.

Approval

In this case the art director was happy with the rough and no revisions were necessary. If revisions had been required, Howard would have needed to respond promptly due to the short deadline. The art director would then in turn need to approve these revisions. Once approval was gained, work could begin on the final artwork.

Final artwork

While working on the final artwork, Howard made refinements to the figure and elements and settled on a colour scheme. Once complete, the artwork was scanned in and sent to the art director for the agreed deadline.

Completion

The work was printed in the magazine, offering an aspect of humour and personality to the column.

HOW TO... DECORATE
Guy Browning

Decorations are what military types get for acts of valour. The more you get, the more colourful your uniform becomes. Some armed forces don't bother with the valour and concentrate on the decorative effect. This external decoration is often seen as a marker of manliness, whereas interior decoration is not. In a way, it's a shame there are no medals for interior decoration.

Decoration is first cousin to elaboration and glorification. It's often seen as bordering on the sinful. Religious sects tend to promote the unadorned look, often because it's cheaper. The richer the sect, the more it tends towards the baroque.

Mankind seems to have an instinct for personal decoration, probably because the genitalia are virtually worthless as plumage. You'll notice peacocks don't bother with cave paintings. Decoration is cultural urination. It's how you mark your territory and warn others not to impose their aesthetic values near your own. An impressionist print on the wall is just an externalised tattoo without the painful piercing.

Humans must find decoration deeply pleasing, because it wasn't long after early humanoids first picked up a stick to use as a tool that they felt the need to whittle it into an owl. Nowadays, it's estimated that more people are involved in the decorative arts than in the martial arts. The two are rarely done hand in hand, although a quick chop through an exquisitely decorated raspberry pavlova is one of life's essential experiences.

In our indoors world, clothing is personal decoration. It is exterior interior design, except that others have to live with it, rather than you. Make-up and jewellery are additional layers of personal decoration. Earrings are the light fittings of the head. Rings are the mantelpiece adornments of the body. Eyebrow shaping is the equivalent of feng shui in that virtually invisible adjustments can have a remarkable effect on the local environment.

MySpace has given a whole new arena for personal decoration. These online bedrooms are decorated to such an amazing degree that it actually becomes unnecessary to exist as a person. Like the peacock, you end up continually showing your plumage to everyone and forgetting how to fly.

6.4

Try it yourself...

Production

Resources and references are essential to every illustrator. With the evolution of the Internet and easily accessible printed material, resources have never been easier to access. Although material is widely available, it is important to develop your own resources through your sketchbooks. This exercise will help you to develop this skill of reference and resource gathering.

Materials

Sketchbook, drawing materials, tape, camera.

The brief: Visiting your local area

Visit a local museum and take your sketchbook with you. Many illustrators use their personal sketchbooks as scrapbooks and as a portable reference. When you visit the museum, have a look around at the objects. Spend time drawing aspects of these preserved artefacts. It may be that you are inspired by the patterns on fabric, or the faces on old painted pottery. Whatever inspires you, draw it! Taking photos is a good way to record things quickly but this is no substitute for the act of drawing. When we draw in our sketchbooks, we will always remember the time, the place, the smells – it is so much more than the pressing of a button.

You may need to visit more than once to allow time to capture all the artefacts that caught your attention. Always have a sketchbook handy as you never know when you may see something that catches your eye and that may be in your next illustration!

You could also visit car boot sales or flea markets to see what interesting items you can find that may inspire you.

Questions in summary

1. What sort of production issues might an illustrator face?
2. Where can illustrators go to find inspiration and factual information?
3. How should a workspace be set up so that it is safe and comfortable?
4. What precautions can an illustrator take to protect against legal and financial difficulties?

1. The illustrator as artist 2. The medium is the message 3. From outcomes to outlets 4. Communicating ideas 5. Making it happen

← Try it yourself... Questions in summary

Contacts

Billie-Jean
www.billiejean.co.uk

Mark Boardman
www.mark-boardman.com

Petra Börner
www.petraborner.com

Anthony Burrill
www.anthonyburrill.com

Annelie Carlström
www.anneliecarlstrom.se
www.anneliecarlstrom.blogspot.com
www.woo.se
www.agencyrush.com

Trina Dalziel
www.trinadalziel.com

Ian Dodds
www.iandodds.co.uk

Miles Donovan
www.milesdonovan.co.uk
www.peepshow.org.uk
www.blackconvoy.com
www.art-dept.com

Tom Duxbury
www.eastwing.co.uk

Sara Fanelli
www.sarafanelli.com

Louise Fenton
www.louisefenton.co.uk

Jason Ford
www.heartagency.com

Maria Forrester
www.mariaillustrator.blogspot.com

Pete Fowler
www.monsterism.net

Blair Frame
www.blairframe.co.uk

Damian Gascoigne
www.eastwing.co.uk

Han Hoogerbrugge
www.hoogerbrugge.com

Margaret Huber
www.margarethuber.com

Insect
www.insect.co.uk

Sarah Jennings
http://sarahj2810.tumblr.com

Adrian Johnson
www.adrianjohnson.org.uk
www.centralillustration.com
www.blackconvoy.com

Matt Jones
http://mattjonesillustration.daportfolio.com

Ben Kelly
www.benkellyland.co.uk

Olivier Kugler
www.olivierkugler.com

Chrissie Macdonald
www.chrissiemacdonald.co.uk
www.peepshow.org.uk

McFaul
www.mcfaul.biz
www.centralillustration.com
www.ba-reps.com
www.blackconvoy.com

Roderick Mills
www.heartagency.com

Mr Bingo
www.mr-bingo.co.uk

Mia Nilsson
www.mianilsson.com
www.woo.se
www.picassopictures.com

Henry Obasi
www.henryobasi.com
www.ppaint.net

Pinky
www.misterpinks.com

Andrew Rae
www.andrewrae.org.uk
www.peepshow.org.uk
www.blackconvoy.com

Howard Read
www.eastwing.co.uk

Kustaa Saksi
www.kustaasaksi.com

Tado
mikeandkatie@tado.co.uk

Jack Taylor
http://cargocollective.com/jtdesign/filter/Illustration

Will Tomlinson
www.williamtomlinson.com

Tim Vyner
www.timvyner.com

Akira Wakui
www.wakuiweb.com

Autumn Whitehurst
www.awhitehurst.com

Ian Wright
www.mrianwright.co.uk

Bibliography

The Beatles Illustrated Lyrics
Alan Aldridge
Little, Brown

The Big Book of Illustration Ideas
Roger Walton
Harper Design International

*Clin D-Oeil – A New Look at Modern
Illustration*
Adam Pointer
Book Industry Services (BIS)

*The Complete Guide to Digital
Illustration*
Steve Caplin and Adam Banks
Ilex

Contact Illustrators and Visionists
Nicholas Gould
Elfande

*Digital Illustration – A Masterclass in
Creative Image-Making*
Lawrence Zeegen
RotoVision

The Education of the Illustrator
Steven Heller and Marshall Arisman
Allworth Press and the School of the
Visual Arts

Fashion Illustration Next
Laird Borrelli
Thames & Hudson

Fashion Illustration Now
Laird Borrelli
Thames & Hudson

The Fundamentals of Creative Design
Gavin Ambrose and Paul Harris
AVA Publishing SA

Hand to Eye – Contemporary Illustration
Angus Hyland and Roanne Bell
Laurence King Publishing

*Head Heart and Hips – The Seductive
World of Big Active*
Gerald Saint
Die Gestalten Verlag

*Imagemakers – Cutting Edge
Fashion Illustration*
Martin Dawber
Mitchell Beazley

*Pen and Mouse – Commercial Art
and Digital Illustration*
Angus Hyland
Laurence King Publishing

Pictoplasma
Peter Thaler
Die Gestalten Verlag

Pictoplasma 2
Peter Thaler
Die Gestalten Verlag

*Picture Perfect – Fusions of
Illustration and Design*
Ian Noble
RotoVision

*Rewind – Forty Years of Design and
Advertising*
Jeremy Myerson and Graham Vickers
Phaidon Press Limited

The Visual Dictionary of Illustration
Mark Williams
AVA Publishing SA

Selected websites

Organizations

House of Illustration (UK)
www.houseofillustration.org.uk

Illustration Friday (UK and USA)
www.illustrationfriday.com

Illustration Mundo (worldwide)
www.illustrationmundo.com

Illustrators' Partnership of America
(USA)
www.illustratorspartnership.org

La Maison des Artistes (France)
www.lamaisondesartistes.fr

The Association of Illustrators (UK)
www.theaoi.com

The Graphic Artists' Guild (USA)
www.graphicartistsguild.org

The Society of Artists' Agents (UK)
www.saahub.com

The Society of Illustrators (USA)
www.societyillustrators.org

The Society of Publication Designers
(USA)
www.spd.org

Tokyo Illustrators' Society (Japan)
en.tis-home.com

Urban sketchers (worldwide)
www.urbansketchers.org

Agencies

Advocate Art (London)
www.advocate-art.com

Agency Rush (London)
www.agencyrush.com

Central Illustration Agency (London)
www.centralillustration.com

Debut Art (London, New York, Paris)
www.debutart.com

Dutch Uncle (London, New York,
Tokyo)
www.dutchuncle.co.uk

Eastwing (London)
www.eastwing.co.uk

Eye Candy (London, New York)
www.eyecandy.co.uk

Heart Agency (London, New York)
www.heartagency.com

Sugar (Tokyo)
www.sugarinc.net

Traffic (New York)
wwww.trafficnyc.com

Annuals

3x3
www.3x3mag.com

American Illustration
www.ai-ap.com

AOI Images
www.aoiimages.com

Communication Arts
www.commarts.com

Creative Handbook
www.chb.com

Creative Review Annual
www.creativereview.co.uk/the-annual

D&AD Annual
www.dandad.org

Directory of Illustration
www.directoryofillustration.com

Le Book
www.lebook.com

Lüerzer's 200 Best Illustrators Worldwide
www.luerzersarchive.net

The Artbook
www.theartbook.com

The Black Book
www.blackbookmag.com

The I-Spot
www.theispot.com

Workbook
www.workbook.com

Glossary

Advertising

A creative and commercial field in which artists, designers and illustrators may be asked to produce work that will help clients to see a service or product to an intended audience.

Agent

An individual or organization formally authorised to represent an artist or illustrator. An agent will promote, secure and conduct business negotiations on behalf of the artist in return for a fee or commission.

Animation

An illusion of movement, created by sequences of images or illustrations. Techniques employed might include, 2D, 3D, claymation, stop-motion and digitally filmed.

Annuals

Yearly catalogues of illustrators and their work. Annuals are distributed to art directors, art buyers and designers for promotional purposes. Some popular illustration annuals are listed on page 171.

Art director

The person who oversees the visual appearance and production of a publishing, film or advertising campaign. The art director will usually work with illustrators, designers, copywriters and editors to ensure the smooth running and aesthetic quality of a project.

Art school

A school, college or higher education establishment that offers educational courses in the visual arts such as photography, sculpture, drawing, painting, illustration, fashion and digital media.

Brainstorm

A problem-solving process whereby large numbers of ideas and thoughts are generated, recorded and sketched. Various techniques, such as image/word associations, similes, spider diagrams and mind maps, can all be used to help keep ideas and thoughts coming.

Brief

Preparatory instructions given to an illustrator, designer or artist embarking on a new project. The brief should detail the objective of the commission, as well as the technical information.

Character

An illustration that portrays human features. Characters in an illustration can be developed to help the audience to engage with the artwork.

Client

An individual or organization paying for the services or work of another individual or organization. In illustration, the client may be a major advertising company or an individual graphic designer.

Collaboration

The bringing together of skills from a variety of professionals. Collaborations between artists can lead to exciting new ideas and boundary-breaking work.

Diagram

A drawing or illustration, used to represent how something works. It may show the parts of a whole and how these parts interact. Diagrams might take the form of pie charts, cut-aways, maps, graphs and plans.

Digital

In illustration, the use of computers and electronic equipment to create an artwork. Illustrators can now create work using a number of digital tools, such as hand-held devices, cameras, tablets and scanners.

Flyers

Small, hand-held marketing materials that are designed to promote events and products. Flyers can be a great way for illustrators to gain exposure.

Graffiti

Painting, carving, scrawling or drawing on walls and objects in public areas. Often with a political or social message, graffiti has been used as an act of protest for many hundreds of years.

Graphic design

The use of text and image to create a visual message. Encompassing typography, layout and image, graphic design work can be used in packaging, advertising, magazines, books, newspapers, animation, signage, web design and branding.

Inspiration

Anything that can trigger a thought or idea, which can form the basis of an artistic concept. Inspiration can be found anywhere, from visiting an antiques fair, to travelling abroad.

Interpretation

The process of translating and explaining something. Interpretation is subjective and will form the basis of most illustration work.

Juxtaposition

The arrangement of elements, side-by-side, in order to highlight differences and similarities. Juxtaposition can be a highly effective tool in illustration and design, creating all sorts of meanings and associations.

Logo

A brand or visual mark, used for identification. Illustrators are often involved in creating logos and brands as their work offers a chance for a unique visual identity.

Mark making

The process of creating outlines and visual representations, using a tool. Mark making is at the heart of all illustration.

Observational drawing

Drawing from real life. Observational drawing requires the illustrator to translate what is seen by the eye into a two-dimensional representation, using line, tone and form.

Photography

The capture of light, in order to reproduce a visual scene. Photography is regularly used and referenced by illustrators in both creating and promoting their work.

Photomontage

A composite image, comprising photography, illustration and other found artwork.

Raster

An image made of pixels. Rasters have a fixed resolution so cannot be enlarged beyond their original size.

Reportage

A type of visual communication, whereby real events are monitored and documented so as to report on and record real-life events.

Sketchbook

A type of visual journal, in which the illustrator or artist can record ideas, thoughts, doodles, inspiration, found materials and notes. The sketchbook is one of the illustrator's most vital pieces of kit.

Storyboard

The act of planning out a sequence or series of visual representations. Storyboarding is used in animation and film-making in particular.

Style

The individual feel or look of an illustrator or artist's work, which distinguishes it from others'. Every illustrator will have their own style and it is this that will help to make work appeal to clients. But remember, styles change and are always subject to trends and fashion!

Technical illustration

Accurate visual representation of a 3D object. Technical illustrations should be as true to life as possible and should be drawn to scale.

Vector

An image that contains scalable objects defined by a mathematical formula. Vectors are resolution independent so can be enlarged without loss of quality.

Index

Page references in *italics* denote illustrations.

Acknowledgements

The publisher would like to thank all the talented people who kindly contributed work to the first edition, and allowed it to be re-used here:

Billie-Jean
Anthony Burrill
Miles Donovan
Sara Fanelli
Jason Ford
Pete Fowler
Han Hoogerbrugge
Margaret Huber
Insect
Adrian Johnson
Chrissie Macdonald
McFaul
Roderick Mills
Mr Bingo
Henry Obasi
Chris Pelling
Pinky
Andrew Rae
Carl Rush
Kustaa Saksi
Tado
Will Tomlinson
Akira Wakui
Autumn Whitehurst
Ian Wright

Thanks also to Mark Boardman, Petra Börner, Annelie Carlström, Tom Duxbury and Mia Nilsson for the work they kindly supplied.

Thanks to Nigel Owen and Rob Brinkerhoff for comments on the manuscript.

Louise Fenton would like to thank all the new contributors to this edition, who have shown that illustration continues to flourish.

Lynne Elvins/Naomi Goulder

Working with ethics

The Fundamentals
of Illustration

The subject of ethics is not new, yet its consideration within the applied visual arts is perhaps not as prevalent as it might be. Our aim here is to help a new generation of students, educators and practitioners find a methodology for structuring their thoughts and reflections in this vital area.

AVA Publishing hopes that these *Working with ethics* pages provide a platform for consideration and a flexible method for incorporating ethical concerns in the work of educators, students and professionals. Our approach consists of four parts:

The *introduction* is intended to be an accessible snapshot of the ethical landscape, both in terms of historical development and current dominant themes.

The *framework* positions ethical consideration into four areas and poses questions about the practical implications that might occur. Marking your response to each of these questions on the scale shown will allow your reactions to be further explored by comparison.

The *case study* sets out a real project and then poses some ethical questions for further consideration. This is a focus point for a debate rather than a critical analysis so there are no predetermined right or wrong answers.

A selection of *further reading* for you to consider areas of particular interest in more detail.

Ethics is a complex subject that interlaces the idea of responsibilities to society with a wide range of considerations relevant to the character and happiness of the individual. It concerns virtues of compassion, loyalty and strength, but also of confidence, imagination, humour and optimism. As introduced in ancient Greek philosophy, the fundamental ethical question is: *what should I do?* How we might pursue a 'good' life not only raises moral concerns about the effects of our actions on others, but also personal concerns about our own integrity.

In modern times the most important and controversial questions in ethics have been the moral ones. With growing populations and improvements in mobility and communications, it is not surprising that considerations about how to structure our lives together on the planet should come to the forefront. For visual artists and communicators, it should be no surprise that these considerations will enter into the creative process.

Some ethical considerations are already enshrined in government laws and regulations or in professional codes of conduct. For example, plagiarism and breaches of confidentiality can be punishable offences. Legislation in various nations makes it unlawful to exclude people with disabilities from accessing information or spaces. The trade of ivory as a material has been banned in many countries. In these cases, a clear line has been drawn under what is unacceptable.

But most ethical matters remain open to debate, among experts and lay-people alike, and in the end we have to make our own choices on the basis of our own guiding principles or values. Is it more ethical to work for a charity than for a commercial company? Is it unethical to create something that others find ugly or offensive?

Specific questions such as these may lead to other questions that are more abstract. For example, is it only effects on humans (and what they care about) that are important, or might effects on the natural world require attention too?

Is promoting ethical consequences justified even when it requires ethical sacrifices along the way? Must there be a single unifying theory of ethics (such as the Utilitarian thesis that the right course of action is always the one that leads to the greatest happiness of the greatest number), or might there always be many different ethical values that pull a person in various directions?

As we enter into ethical debate and engage with these dilemmas on a personal and professional level, we may change our views or change our view of others. The real test though is whether, as we reflect on these matters, we change the way we act as well as the way we think. Socrates, the 'father' of philosophy, proposed that people will naturally do 'good' if they know what is right. But this point might only lead us to yet another question: *how do we know what is right?*

You
What are your ethical beliefs?

Central to everything you do will be your attitude to people and issues around you. For some people, their ethics are an active part of the decisions they make every day as a consumer, a voter or a working professional. Others may think about ethics very little and yet this does not automatically make them unethical. Personal beliefs, lifestyle, politics, nationality, religion, gender, class or education can all influence your ethical viewpoint.

Using the scale, where would you place yourself? What do you take into account to make your decision? Compare results with your friends or colleagues.

Your client
What are your terms?

Working relationships are central to whether ethics can be embedded into a project, and your conduct on a day-to-day basis is a demonstration of your professional ethics. The decision with the biggest impact is whom you choose to work with in the first place. Cigarette companies or arms traders are often-cited examples when talking about where a line might be drawn, but rarely are real situations so extreme. At what point might you turn down a project on ethical grounds and how much does the reality of having to earn a living affect your ability to choose?

Using the scale, where would you place a project? How does this compare to your personal ethical level?

01 02 03 04 05 06 07 08 09 10

01 02 03 04 05 06 07 08 09 10

Your specifications
What are the impacts of your materials?

In relatively recent times, we are learning that many natural materials are in short supply. At the same time, we are increasingly aware that some man-made materials can have harmful, long-term effects on people or the planet. How much do you know about the materials that you use? Do you know where they come from, how far they travel and under what conditions they are obtained? When your creation is no longer needed, will it be easy and safe to recycle? Will it disappear without a trace? Are these considerations your responsibility or are they out of your hands?

Using the scale, mark how ethical your material choices are.

Your creation
What is the purpose of your work?

Between you, your colleagues and an agreed brief, what will your creation achieve? What purpose will it have in society and will it make a positive contribution? Should your work result in more than commercial success or industry awards? Might your creation help save lives, educate, protect or inspire? Form and function are two established aspects of judging a creation, but there is little consensus on the obligations of visual artists and communicators toward society, or the role they might have in solving social or environmental problems. If you want recognition for being the creator, how responsible are you for what you create and where might that responsibility end?

Using the scale, mark how ethical the purpose of your work is.

01 02 03 04 05 06 07 08 09 10

01 02 03 04 05 06 07 08 09 10

One aspect of illustration that raises an ethical dilemma is that of creating satirical drawings which can depict people in fictional situations. In satire, issues are ridiculed or derided and although a sketch is usually meant to be funny, the purpose is often to attack something that the illustrator disapproves of. Cruel caricatures and exaggeration can be used both to amuse and to encourage debate. Sometimes, the more ridiculous an illustration becomes, the better it can be at raising a point and making viewers think – political cartoons are one example. But what is funny and thought-provoking to one person can very often be highly offensive and infuriating to another. Is it up to an illustrator to know the difference between intelligent provocation and extreme bad taste, or should viewers accept that satirical illustrations must cause offence in some form if they are to fulfil their role?

In 1953, the US Senate Subcommittee to Investigate Juvenile Delinquency formed to consider the causes of juvenile crime. In 1954, it opened hearings looking specifically at the influences of the comic book industry. In evidence against comic books, various storylines were exhibited, for example, children killing their parents and grossly deformed women. Critic Fredrick Wertham appeared before the committee stating that 'as long as the crime comic book industry exists… there are no secure homes'. It was concluded that there was not a deliberate attempt among publishers to promote such content. Instead, they were driven by fulfilling demand and the pursuit of profit.

While the subcommittee adjourned, civic groups, retailers and other politicians urged the industry to clean up its own act. In response, all but three publishers formed the Comics Magazine Association of America (CMAA) and appointed Charles F Murphy as the 'comics czar'. His job was to create and enforce a code of standards to regain public trust.

The new standards forbade showing any sympathy towards criminal activity and declared that no disrespect could be shown towards authorities or institutions. It banned the words 'horror' and 'terror' from appearing on covers and strictly disallowed insults or attacks on religious or racial groups. Women were not to be drawn in 'salacious' dress. In these and other ways, the CMAA publicly declared its moral responsibility for American youth. In 1955, the Senate Subcommittee published its own conclusions and resolved to keep a watchful eye on the CMAA code. By 1956, controversy over comic book content had effectively ended and concerns over juvenile delinquency shifted to television, film and rock and roll.

The code was unexpectedly revised in 1970 after The Department of Health, Education and Welfare asked Marvel Comics to incorporate an anti-drugs storyline in one of its titles. In the story, Peter Parker's friend starts taking drugs and Peter confronts the dealers; Spider-Man saves the man 'stoned right out of his mind' after he walks off a building thinking that he can fly. But the CMAA code did not allow any depiction of drugs and therefore it did not gain immediate approval. Despite this, Marvel published the story. It proved to be a best-seller and consequently, the code was revised to reflect the attitudes of the more liberal reading public.

Is it unethical to illustrate criminal activity?

Do codes of practice make professions more ethical?

Would you illustrate a government publication?

I prefer drawing to talking. Drawing is faster, and leaves less room for lies.

Le Corbusier

AIGA
Design Business and Ethics
2007, AIGA

Eaton, Marcia Muelder
Aesthetics and the Good Life
1989, Associated University Press

Ellison, David
Ethics and Aesthetics in European Modernist Literature:
From the Sublime to the Uncanny
2001, Cambridge University Press

Fenner, David E W (Ed)
Ethics and the Arts:
An Anthology
1995, Garland Reference Library of Social Science

Gini, Al and Marcoux, Alexei M
Case Studies in Business Ethics
2005, Prentice Hall

McDonough, William and Braungart, Michael
Cradle to Cradle:
Remaking the Way We Make Things
2002, North Point Press

Papanek, Victor
Design for the Real World:
Making to Measure
1972, Thames & Hudson

United Nations Global Compact
The Ten Principles
www.unglobalcompact.org/AboutTheGC/TheTenPrinciples/index.html